DARK TOURIST

21st Century Essays
David Lazar and Patrick Madden, Series Editors

Dark Tourist

ESSAYS

Hasanthika Sirisena

MAD CREEK BOOKS, AN IMPRINT OF
THE OHIO STATE UNIVERSITY PRESS
COLUMBUS

Library of Congress Cataloging-in-Publication Data
Names: Sirisena, Hasanthika, author.
Title: Dark tourist : essays / Hasanthika Sirisena.
Other titles: 21st century essays.
Description: Columbus : Mad Creek Books, an imprint of The Ohio State University Press [2021] | Series: 21st century essays | Includes bibliographical references. | Summary: "Blends reportage, cultural criticism, and memoir to excavate sites of personal, cultural, and political trauma and find wider truths about sexuality, art, language, and identity"—Provided by publisher.
Identifiers: LCCN 2021023149 | ISBN 9780814258125 (paperback) | ISBN 0814258123 (paperback) | ISBN 9780814281697 (ebook) | ISBN 0814281699 (ebook)
Subjects: LCSH: Sirisena, Hasanthika. | LCGFT: Essays.
Classification: LCC PS3619.I752 D37 2021 | DDC 814/.6—dc23
LC record available at https://lccn.loc.gov/2021023149

Cover design and illustration by Caitlin Sacks, Notch Design
Text design by Juliet Williams
Type set in Adobe Garamond Pro

CONTENTS

ACKNOWLEDGMENTS

To Kristen Elias Rowley, David Lazar, and everyone at Mad Creek Books and The Ohio State University Press for shepherding this book.

To Patrick Madden for your deep care and humanity.

To the following magazines for publishing my work: "Broken Arrow," *Copper Nickel*; "Lady," *The Arkansas International*; "Confessions of a Dark Tourist," *Michigan Quarterly Review*; "Pretty Girl Murdered," *WSQ*; "In the Presence of God I Make This Vow," *Kenyon Review Online*; "Abecedarian for the Abeyance of Loss," *Epiphany*.

To the editors: Caroline Beimford, Geoffrey Brock, Jonathan Freedman, Geeta Kothari, Rachel Lyon, Joanna Luloff, Kami Wicoff.

To my agent Kate Johnson for all your advice.

To my friends who read and supported these essays in their fledgling states: V. V. Ganeshananthan, Philip Metres, Heidi Schwegler, Wendy S. Walters, G. C. Waldrep.

To my students and colleagues at the Vermont College of Fine Arts and Susquehanna University for the inspiration.

To the Virginia Center for the Creative Arts for giving me time and space.

To Tomás Q. Morín, my brother in arms, for keeping me afloat.

To Joel Holub for holding me against the sorrow and the rage and giving far more than I deserved.

To my family in Sri Lanka for giving me a home.

To my sisters and brother (in-law) for your brilliance and for putting up with me.

To my niece and nephew. I love you both more than anything.

To thatha, for bringing me here and believing I could do this.

Most of all to my mother. I told your story, mommy. I told it straight.

PART 1

LOSS . . .

Broken Arrow

1961

On January 22, along the coast of North Carolina, the eight-man crew of a B-52 realizes their plane is losing fuel too fast. The right wing might be damaged but there's no way for them to check. Only two members of the crew can see outside, and all that is visible to either of them is the night sky and the ocean: a purple-red bruise intersecting at the horizon. The pilot, Major Tulloch, radios Seymour Johnson Air Force Base in Goldsboro, North Carolina, that the plane must make an emergency landing. This wouldn't be particularly notable except that the *Keep-19* mission is part of the Strategic Air Command and is on a test run for a program meant to allow the United States to be the first to attack in case of a nuclear war. The plane carries two Mark 39 thermonuclear weapons, in other words two hydrogen bombs. Both of these bombs together have an explosive yield 500 times greater than the bomb that destroyed Hiroshima and a kill range of somewhere between seven and eight and a half miles. Each is active, ready to detonate upon being dropped.

The January night is cold and, because of a front moving through, the air at that altitude is estimated at 150 knots. (A Category 1 hurricane measures winds of 62 to 82 knots). During the second mid-air refueling the turbulence is so strong Tulloch struggles to keep the plane steady. He feels every buffet and pitch in his muscles, in his bones. The cockpit of the bomber is not a comfortable place. It is all metal and glass and smells of sweat, burnt rubber, and urine. The crew has been on alert, not just for the ten-hour flying time, but also before that on the ground as they waited hours to receive their commands. They are, by now, simultaneously tired and wired, fueled by adrenaline and raw desire to complete the mission. At some point during the refueling, the pilot reportedly asks a co-pilot to hand-fly the plane so he can rest a moment. It takes at least three tries to finish what should be a simple process.

Flying a plane takes strength, coordination, and mental stamina under any circumstance. B-52 Stratofortresses are massive planes; 200 tons of metal, a wingspan of over 180 feet, eight engines. In the sky, these are the hulking monsters of war movies, casting long shadows that slide menacingly across fields and mountains. On the runway, the bulk slows the bomber down and causes it to waddle as it accelerates—ground crews dub the lumbering procession the elephant walk. The standard instrument panel consists of eight throttles and thirty-two gauges for monitoring the engines.

But I am not being fair when I reconstruct this plane using only bolts and metal plates, tonnage and turbo-power. The B-52 is surprisingly sensitive, with a delicately balanced central nervous system dedicated ultimately to maintaining life. I am always shocked when I read about plane crashes (as I like to do) to realize that planes aren't built to beat nature—nothing manmade can at an altitude of 40,000 feet—but to defy it, like an extended and especially precarious game of tiddlywinks.

Major Tulloch is a career soldier with the thick, beefy features of an extra in a World War II re-enactment. He enlisted after Pearl Harbor at the age of twenty-nine and has served ever since, first as a soldier and later as a fighter pilot and a test pilot. He has hundreds of hours of combat experience and has walked away from three test plane crashes. He is by military standards an old man at forty-six and at least a decade and a half older than most of the crew. But he is the sort of man SAC wants flying these missions: seasoned, tough, capable.

He is not afraid when the crew reports that they have lost nineteen tons of fuel in little under two minutes. He does not imagine as I do some dumb, dinosaur-like beast, suspended high above, beyond our ken, bleeding out, slowly dying. He does not feel that frisson of excitement, that metallic taste on the tongue, at the thought of some great catastrophe. He is too professional to indulge imagination. He listens instead as the *Addle 57*, the fuel tanker, informs him they have spotted the leak at the base of the right wing. He knows he and his crew are in some danger, though he does not know how much. He also understands that with that much fuel, with that much weight, they cannot land or the plane will break apart. They must stay aloft. He does as he is commanded: he moves the plane several hundred miles off the coast of Wilmington to prevent, if they do have to crash-land, possible nuclear destruction.

1975

A few months into his first job in America, at Cherry Hospital in Goldsboro, my father is assigned a new patient, a paranoid schizophrenic, who everyone else in his unit is afraid of. According to my father, he had grown up in Brooklyn and served time in New York State for assaulting a man. When the state released the patient from Sing Sing, the corrections officer gave him a bus ticket and told him to travel as far away as possible. He made it to North Carolina before voices instructed him to stab a man in a bus terminal restroom. The day of his release from the North Carolina correctional facility, the patient refused to leave. The guards turned a high-pressure water hose on him to blast him from his cell and admitted him to Cherry Hospital because, as his court-appointed lawyer put it, "You had to be crazy not to want to leave jail."

The patient is a small man, lithe but powerful. He is Black. Unlike many of the other patients at Cherry Hospital who take little interest in their personal hygiene, he dresses in neatly kept, well-fitting clothes. The orderlies and nurses are afraid of him and refuse to get on an elevator alone with him, claiming he hides a shank somewhere on his body. Behind his back, they make fun of his composure, call him "queer."

According to my father, no one else wants to take this man on as a patient, and he doesn't really have a choice either. I wonder, when my father tells me this, if he wasn't assigned the patient as some sort of punishment. My father, all his life, has elicited from others respect for his intelligence and confidence, and the desire to put him in his place. The latter he brings on himself. He is charming but also quick-tempered, often rude and abrasive with little warning.

During the interview, my father watches the patient closely. He appears calm, almost listless, and he doesn't make eye contact. He is thirty-eight, making him and my father close to each other in age. But this man before my father is alone—with any family long ago lost to him—and very ill. He keeps his hands on the table in front of him where everyone can see them, another sign of life spent in institutions.

My father asks if he knows what the following proverb means: a watched pot never boils. The patient takes a long time to respond. When he finally does, he speaks to the corner of the room. He explains that if you watch a pot the water won't boil.

This isn't an indication of the man's intelligence but a symptom, instead, of his disease. He prefers, perhaps can only comprehend, the literal. His mind cannot contend with the deeper, figurative meaning.

My father notes the response on the patient's chart. When he looks back, he is distracted momentarily by some feeling of sorrow. He isn't supposed to be here, he thinks. He is here by accident. He's very well-prepared and very ambitious. He left Sri Lanka in the early '70s to complete a prestigious fellowship in England. He was supposed to arrive in a New World, but this world, rendered barren by the cool October wind, looks anything but new. The fields with their hardened dark earth and desiccated cornstalks are used and unpromising. Cherry Hospital feels worn and tired with its decades-old brick buildings. In movies, on television, American hospitals had looked bright, all white, with young and attractive nurses and doctors. Cherry Hospital reeks of ammonia and mildew.

The patient complains of pain in his arm and shoulder. Last week, my father and the patient had had a lively conversation about boxing. Both were boxers in their youth, and they bonded over this shared interest. But the patient isn't lively today. This might be the pain; it might be the Haldol. He begins to explain that the pain is caused by radio waves, emitted by a transmitter at Seymour Johnson Air Force Base. This is a man whose brain has splintered, a brain that doesn't properly process sensory information. It doesn't process social cues. His victim at the bus terminal may have taunted him or he may have smiled.

I learn all this during a series of interviews I conduct with my father for a novel that I never published. My father also explains to me that the lawyer was wrong. This patient wasn't "crazy" for not wanting to leave jail. According to my father, mentally ill patients often seek the comfort and shelter of a rigorously structured environment. It eases the confusion and disorientation. My father speaks solemnly, his expression is one of compassion.

This is the only patient my father has *ever* spoken about to me and I'm struck by the way the man stays with my father and bothers him. He is one of the reasons that my father—who became certified to practice both psychiatry and general medicine—decided to leave psychiatry and build instead an internal medicine practice. I don't know why, out of the hundreds of patients my father treated in his forty-year career, this patient stays with him. He does reveal the complete diagnosis: paranoid schizophrenia due to socio-cultural deprivation.

"We thought it was a joke," my father says to me. By "we" he means his colleagues at the hospital, many who were immigrants as well. "The diagnoses we were making. Socio-cultural deprivation! We'd never heard of that diagnosis in England."

I didn't really understand what this might have meant to my father until recently. I was trying to explain to my new boss, a South African who immigrated to the States in his twenties, what it was like to grow up in the South. I mentioned my father's anger about the diagnoses. My boss cocked his head and thought about this for a moment. Then he added, "That must have been something for your father, coming from where he did."

I shook my head, not understanding. My boss smiled gently. "Your father thinks he's coming to the first world, to modernization. Instead he finds socio-cultural deprivation." When I still didn't quite get it, my boss added, "Your father replaced one third-world experience for another."

The Crash

Somewhere close to midnight, the *Keep-19* crew is told to return to Seymour Johnson Air Force Base. No one truly knows the extent of the structural damage to the wing, but another B-52 in a similar situation had landed safely. They are landing in Goldsboro, not out at sea, because the military does not want to lose their expensive payload to the ocean. Two hydrogen bombs are not an easy loss to explain, and the operations are only in their testing phases. That these military strategists did not quantify or identify the extraordinary destruction that would take place if one of those bombs detonated over Goldsboro is profoundly disturbing. These are the same men who can imagine, quantify, extrapolate, demonstrate the massive loss of life and destruction that would take place if Russia dropped a bomb on us. They seem not to understand that, at this moment, the biggest threat comes from within.

Air traffic control clears the *Keep-19* mission crew to land at Seymour Johnson Air Force Base. They wish the crew luck, an acknowledgement that everyone on the ground understands the plane is in danger. The crew is able to lower the landing gear and the wing flaps without incident. Major Tulloch positions them to land. But, the plane continues to turn on its own. The copilots stomp the rudder pedals, pull the control wheel hard left. Their muscles twitch and pop with the effort. The acid burn of near exhaustion floods their bodies, but they have trained themselves not to give in. These efforts aren't enough. The plane barrel rolls. The crew hears and feels the explosion, then realizes the right wing has snapped off. What starts as a crack becomes, through the forces of physics and nature, a splintering and then a shattering as if 200 tons of steel and wire is nothing more than a plate being knocked from a table or a mirror loosened from its wall mount.

Major Tulloch gives the command to the crew to bail. Their response is not the terror-stricken, catastrophic hysteria depicted in movie plane crashes. They are trained for this and remain calm. One crewmember asks Tulloch to repeat his command because he isn't sure he's heard correctly. "Bail out,"

Tulloch insists with more urgency. Only six of the eight crew members can use ejector seats. The extras must make their way to an escape hatch on the lower level in the belly of the plane. A copilot, Lieutenant Adam Mattocks, removes his headset and unbuckles his seatbelt. When he tries to stand, the g-force slams him backward with such force that he blacks out. When he recovers consciousness, he sees Tulloch struggling violently, and vainly, to maintain control of the plane as it descends.

Mattocks realizes he cannot make it to the lower level and that he most likely going to die. He attempts a maneuver no one has survived: he bails, without an ejector seat, from an open overhead hatch. He's lucky—very lucky. Because the plane is spinning, the overhead hatch is no longer overhead but instead positioned to the left. He doesn't fall onto the plane or any of its wreckage but free of it. He describes a moment of inertia—of being suspended. It must have been beautiful in its awfulness. This plane spiraling as Mattocks somersaults in tandem: metal and flesh silhouetted against a perfect, yellow pinhole moon.

A Roll of the Dice

In the past few years, we've spoken so much about Goldsboro that I can easily imagine life for my father back then. I can invoke my father as he finishes his breakfast—sardines on toast and a cup of milk tea. I can hear the sirens wail. Many of the employees of Cherry Hospital live in housing provided by the hospital. The siren—heard across the campus—marks the change from the evening shift to the morning.

He swipes the corners of his mouth with a napkin, stands, and makes his way from the dining room to the front door where his coat—his favorite tweed blazer that he bought from Marks & Spencer in London—is hanging. He passes me seated on the floor, cross-legged, eating a bowl of cereal and watching the *Uncle Paul Show*. A grown man in a top hat marches a gaggle of children in a circle in time to some inane children's song. I am riveted, absolutely enthralled and do not register my father's presence in the room. When, he wonders, have they begun allowing me to eat breakfast in front of the television? He hears my mother in the bedroom getting dressed so that she can walk me to school. The idea overwhelms him that he is making some sort of mistake. He has brought his family into a world that, despite his considerable intelligence, he cannot decode or comprehend, and when he tries to sleep at night his mind somersaults envisioning failure after failure.

He claimed, many times during my childhood, he really wanted a job in New Zealand. The hospital was interested, and New Zealand and Australia heavily recruited doctors like my father. In his re-telling he doesn't get the New Zealand job because his boss in London decided not to mail his recommendation. My father didn't want to return to Sri Lanka because of the political turmoil and because he felt there was little opportunity for him there. My father accepted the post at Cherry Hospital after interviewing for the position in London, and he took the job without visiting the hospital or North Carolina before arriving.

My father confessed recently that if he'd known what North Carolina was going to be like he wouldn't have come. I asked him why he decided to stay then. At first, when things were the worst, he didn't have the money to return. Later, he didn't want to wrench us, his daughters, from the home we knew. Eventually, he came to like his patients, and he thought he was serving them in some way. "But I wouldn't have believed that at first," he admitted. "For a long time, I knew I had made a mistake."

I am not trying to compare my father's immigration— which was, in fact a success given his successful medical career and his loving family—to a plane crash. Perhaps it's my age or where I am in my life, but I am fascinated by the calculations we make, the line between triumph and failure. What I know about probability I know from my dad, who loved mathematics, and studied it, as a hobby, all his life. And what I know is that the study of probability, statistics, is the study, ultimately, of how we think and reason. The mathematician Pierre-Simon Laplace marks induction—drawing a particular conclusion from many outcomes—as a major moment of progress in science, math, morality, and justice. As he notes in his *A Philosophical Essay on Probability*, we are afraid of the comet the first time we see it, believe it is the cause of the fall of an empire. By the fourth revolution, though, we have come to understand the laws of nature and we understand that our comet is not at all connected to our fate. He also acknowledges that if human reason is dependent on inductive reasoning then "almost all our knowledge is only probable."

Laplace imagines a being who knows everything, all the forces of nature and therefore the cause and effect of all actions: "For such an intellect nothing would be uncertain and the future just like the past would be present before its eyes." Laplace's demon is god-like without the beneficence or humanity we tend to ascribe to God; he is also, as I read Laplace, what the human intellect should and can aspire to. Any freshman psychology or philosophy student can rebut Laplace's philosophy, but I am drawn to his elegance and ambition. Laplace believes that science and math—not religion—will one day lead us away from superstition and ignorance and ameliorate the terror that comes from not knowing what will happen next.

But science has not yet delivered on that promise, and we still live with the fear of the imagined probable. Perhaps that explains why my father's love of mathematics—and for making predictions—took an odd turn in the '90s and '00s. He became an astrologer. He'd sit for hours solving equations and charting in elaborate and painstaking detail the positions of planets.

His obsession was in part cultural. Astrology is very important in South Asian culture, and many members of my highly

educated and accomplished family don't act without first con-
sulting an astrologer. The actual system of charting a horoscope
is complicated, involving math and calculation and the exact
position of planets in relation to each other and the earth, an
elaborate system of causation. It's complicated enough to *appear*
a science (and, in fact, in the Greek and ancient Islamic world,
astrologers were also astronomers and mathematicians). I think
that's why astrology appealed to my father. If medicine was
the science that kept pushing him to the West, astrology was the
"science" that kept him rooted in his culture. I remember the
charts he drew, a series of concentric and interconnecting cir-
cles, that resembled, to my untrained eye, spirographs

It's easy to scorn my father's obsession, but instead, I try
to imagine the level of uncertainty he grappled with, from his
life as an immigrant to his career as a doctor. He contended
every day with death, often the deaths of people he'd grown
to like and care about. I really can't begrudge him his desire to
find some way to forestall and to explain the terrible grief he
felt at being displaced, to ease the anxiety of wondering if he
had made a mistake—in a diagnosis, in a cultural slip to a colleague or his own daughter, in leaving his homeland. My father
studied astrology for decades and even became certified by the
American Federation of Astrology. Last summer, when I was
packing up his office, I found the certificate provided by the
AFA framed and hanging on the wall across from all his diplo-
mas and medical certifications, placed so that he would be able
to see it every day from his desk as he worked.

Survivors

Lieutenant Mattocks became the first person to survive a jump
from an overhead hatch of an airplane. Major Tulloch, to the
disbelief of those on the ground, came stumbling out of a
Goldsboro swamp covered in mud, unharmed. Five members

of the crew lived; three died. Even if you've never heard about the Goldsboro "broken arrow," you know the end of this story. The two hydrogen bombs did not detonate, though according to military records one bomb came close. Five of the six arming devices had been activated.

One of the bombs was recovered intact. The second fell into a swamp. The bomb sank deeper into the mud and the military was only able to make a partial retrieval. The rest remains buried in the ground in Faro a few miles from Goldsboro.

The US military created different designations for a variety of potential nuclear incidents. "Broken arrow" is the term for an accidental or near detonation. There have been thirty-two broken arrows globally and three in the United States. My sister sent me a link to the original *Guardian* article, published in 2013, detailing journalist Eric Schlosser's work to uncover more about what happened in Goldsboro. Her accompanying message was one line: *How different our lives would be if the bomb went off and we went back to SL instead of moving to Goldsboro.* Though I recognize it's the human condition to wonder what might have been, it's the immigrant's particular condition to live always with the idea that you might have lived a parallel life, been someone else completely.

I'm awed by the risks our government took, the short-sightedness, the willingness to place us in jeopardy. For all the talk of Russia's threat, we were just as likely—perhaps more likely—to have blown *ourselves* up. Still, any good writing workshop stresses that a tragedy averted does not make for a particularly impactful story. We want weighted consequences to our actions, and if we manage to find our footing in the swamp and stumble out intact, we should pat ourselves on the back and move on.

But what about the verity of those stories we tell ourselves? The stories that buttress our fears and justify the risks we take? I remember *The Day After* and *Red Dawn*. I sang along to the radio, "I hope the Russians love their children too." I remember going to bed believing the Russians would bomb us as I slept. I never knew an American nuclear warhead was buried just miles from my bedroom. No, I wouldn't have slept any better, but I would have known something closer to the truth.

A great many people are constantly taking risks with their lives, with our lives, with my life. Each of us takes our own risks in near darkness. We all might as well be Laplace's primitive man staring at the sky in awe, believing that the comet is an omen.

The Demon

My father assiduously monitored his health his whole life. Diabetes runs in his family, and his father, my grandfather, passed away in his fifties from a heart attack. My father ran. He built a weight room in his basement. He watched his diet. Yet, when his physician suggested he take a blood thinner for his atrial fibrillation he decided against it. He was very healthy, active, and very low risk. He also, given his family history, was more afraid of a heart attack. He believed he would be able to sense an arrhythmia.

He suffered a massive stroke a year ago that left his body partially paralyzed and his brain shattered. He can no longer read. He's easily confused, and he requires twenty-four-hour care. He finds it difficult to speak in English even though before the stroke he was bilingual. I overheard his caretaker the other day carefully explaining the days of the week to him. He regularly mentions a visitor who as far as we can tell doesn't exist. He wants a dog with a childlike fervor, but we can't buy him one because he cannot care for himself much less an animal.

I learned of my father's decision not to take the medicine while he was in the hospital after the stroke. It angers me that my father counted on luck in such a way. I also realize when I second-guess my father's decision, I am pretending at being Laplace's demon. I think about those men at SAC guessing and second-guessing their decisions and recognize I'm engaging in my own strange and clumsy pas de deux with life's events. We can't ever *know*. Arthur Schopenhauer in *World as Will and Presentation* quotes ancient Vedic philosophy when trying to define the mind's relationship to its present: "It is Maya the veil of deception that envelopes the eyes of mortals, lets them see a world of which one can say neither that it is nor that it is not; for it is like a dream, like the reflection of the sun on the sand that the wanderer takes from afar as for water, or a rope thrown down that one sees as a snake."

I don't recognize this man my father has become. I'm guessing he could live like this for a long time, or not, and I'm scared of the future either way. My father doesn't speak much anymore to my sisters or to me because we can't converse in Sinhala. He speaks a great deal to my stepmother. One day, my sister wanted to know what they were talking about. I admitted to eavesdropping. My Sinhala isn't very good, but I think she was telling him stories. The narratives sounded like bedtime stories, and he didn't respond, only listened. After a moment, feeling the intruder, realizing I didn't really understand anyway, I turned and tiptoed away.

Lady

i.

We don't have a name for what is wrong with my mother. We only witness the symptoms. Coughing fits rack my mother's tiny frame. Her body seizes and contorts as she tries to force out the air. She can't breathe and her voice reduces to rasps. She complains of pain, a crescent shaped stabbing sensation at the base of her ribcage. Her eyes water as she wills herself to stop coughing, to stop the involuntary muscle contractions. I watch, helpless each time: a slender, electric wire snakes its way from my gut and coils at the base of my throat, a sensation I associate with empathy. But my mild discomfort does not compare to my mother's visible and considerable pain. I ask if she wants a glass of water. I know the answer. She can't hold a glass steady enough to drink. Water doesn't help anyway, since she finds it hard to swallow between coughs. She wears a diaper because during these coughing bouts she loses control of her bladder and the leaking embarrasses her. Later, I empty from the wastebasket blood-splattered tissues. Their fragile, crumpled remains remind me of decorative carnations.

ii.

The first production of *Lady Windermere's Fan* has finished and the audience cheers and claps. They call Oscar Wilde's name. Outside the St. James' Theatre, the atmosphere is cold, all mist and gloom—characteristically London. On the street, the steady beat, thick and wet, of horse hooves and the trundling of the hansom cabs clogs the night. Inside, the air is crisp, made animate by the hum of electric lights. The bulbs and fixtures exude a blue scent, like chlorine disinfectant, the odor that precedes an electrical storm. This only lends to the feeling of excitement.

As he looks out from the stage, the theater lights blind him. They extend before him, beds of gleaming golden crocuses. Their brilliance makes it impossible for him to see the audience though he knows the theater is filled to capacity. His wife and two former female lovers are there, as well as a group of young men for whom he has procured tickets. He has asked each of these men to wear a green carnation as a sort of a joke, because he enjoys meaningless signs and symbols. In the buttonhole of his own jacket, he sports a carnation painted a vibrant shade of verdigris.

The cheers of the audience turn to hoots. He is loved. He stretches out a hand, sheathed in a mauve glove, cigarette dangling from his fingertips. Bits of ash flake onto the stage. He thanks the actors: "I congratulate you on the great success of your performance which persuades me that you think almost as highly of the play as I do myself."

Lady Windermere's Fan—unlike Wilde's other notable works up to that point, *The Portrait of Dorian Gray* and *Salome*—will win for Wilde acceptance. There *is* criticism, mostly of his after-performance speech. Henry James, never a fan, gripes in a letter: "The unspeakable one had responded to curtain calls by appearing with a metallic blue carnation in his buttonhole and cigarette in his fingers." Later, others will remember and whisper about all the boy-men sporting blue-green carnations: it is meant to signify, they will claim, a certain, peculiar kind of solidarity.

iii.

In the early 1900s, the American poet Ellen Wheeler Wilcox wrote in *National Magazine* about the women she had met on a trip to Ceylon. She notes, admiringly, that these upper-class Ceylonese women are articulate and urbane. She focuses on one in particular: "Mrs. de Mel was educated in the English mission school, and speaks not only her own Singhalese tongue . . . but English and French fluently. . . . Mother of six children, this Singhalese lady takes charge of their education, and looks after their clothing, health, and pleasures while she dispenses large hospitalities . . ."

My mother, born upper-class, in Colombo, some forty years after Mrs. de Mel, was very much a product of this culture of lady-making. She could run a kitchen, sew, dress well, speak well. She acquiesced to an arranged marriage. She knew how to tend to the well-being of another person. Even Wilcox's description of Mrs. de Mel—"Her complexion is soft brown, something like the shade of unburnt coffee, and her long straight hair, clear cut features, and dazzling teeth . . . made her a target for admiring glances"—could just as easily describe my mother.

She loved more than anything else to cook. She made meals for us seven days a week. On at least one Sunday a month, she concocted the elaborate lunches served during her childhood in Sri Lanka: a meat curry, a vegetable curry, dhal, watercress mallung, fried eggplant, papadum, and sometimes, if we were lucky, fish cutlets. She also on the weekends baked pastries and cakes covered in homemade butter icing and powdered sugar.

The elaborate meals, typical to an upper-class family in Sri Lanka, were recreated in detail in our middle-class household in America.

I have a memory of watching her in the kitchen. She spreads her hand out. A band-aid encircles one finger. The pink mesh has turned to rust and the band-aid has become stiff and encrusted. The skin on the top of her hand has become severely dry, split, and cracked. Enough blood has congealed that the entire wound has stopped bleeding, but it hurts my mother to move the finger or to try to grasp the handle of the knife. It also hurts my mother to wash her hands. As soon as she does the water dissolves the crusted blood, and she starts bleeding again.

iv.

The first mention of Lady Windermere syndrome appears in 1992 in the journal *Chest*. The authors of the article noticed the cluster of symptoms in a group of six elderly female patients who each appeared to be trying to suppress their cough. These women must have also appeared exceptionally prim because the authors came to believe the cough suppression might be linked to gender-specific behavior: "The medical apothegm 'Ladies don't spit,' embodies the idea that female patients are more fastidious and hence more likely to regard expectoration as socially unacceptable behavior." According to the authors, they named the syndrome after Lady Windermere because of the character's refusal to shake hands with Lord Darlington in a key scene in the play. (A scene I've not been able to find in the play itself.)

v.

During the last few months of her life, when my mother went to sleep, her breathing became so shallow carbon dioxide built to dangerous levels in her blood and she became hypoxic. She awoke disoriented, suffered memory loss. Sometimes, when the oxygen deprivation reached its worst levels, she hallucinated. She believed once that her father and mother, long deceased, stood next to her bed talking to her. She confided in my father that she continued to hold on to the possibility even when she understood it was a hallucination that her mother and father had, in fact, come to visit her. None of us recognized the degree to which the memory loss was disrupting her daily life until we went through my parents' finances after her death. We realized that bills had gone months unpaid. In some cases, we were weeks away from dealing with a debt collection agency.

My mother relied on a CPAP machine to help oxygenate her blood as she slept. She used a portable unit placed next to her bed every evening. Eventually, the portable CPAP became useless. It wasn't powerful enough to counteract the shallowness of her breathing. She had to go to the hospital more and more frequently. Her greatest fear at that time was that she might be placed on a ventilator, unable to breath on her own. Finally, a few days before she died the doctors told her she could remain on the CPAP for good or be disconnected and die painlessly from the buildup of carbon dioxide in her blood. She chose to be taken off. She told us that she couldn't stand the sound of the CPAP, an omnipresent roaring in her ears that felt to her like being trapped in a wind tunnel. My family and I worried that perhaps she chose to die because she didn't want to inconvenience us by lingering. My mother was like that, always worried about how we were being inconvenienced.

When the nurse removed the CPAP, my mother called her family in Sri Lanka to speak with them. By that time my mother was short of breath and her voice had reduced to a faint growl. Days later, when we called my aunt to tell her my mother had passed, she screamed. My aunt and one of my mother's cousins insist my mother had told them she was going to get better. Maybe my aunt had misunderstood. Maybe she couldn't understand my mother, and allowed herself to believe my mother was saying something else, or maybe in the end, my mother did lie. Maybe my mother wanted to spare her family a few extra days of sorrow.

vi.

My earliest memories are of my mother in hospital. I spent my childhood fearing she was going to die and leave me with a father who felt distant and too often angry at the world and at me. Eventually, without an explanation, without an understanding of what was wrong, that fear curdled into anger at my mother for being endlessly ill.

I'm obsessed with female toughness. This theme spills into my fiction and into my personal choices. This is partly the result of living with my mother's illness. It also comes from being the smallest, weakest child at my school and in my neighborhood. I was timid, easily spooked, and lacking any physical grace or athletic ability.

One day, I was playing with my friends when one of them, Catherine Dunstan, demanded I climb a tree. Even if I had wanted to, I wouldn't have been physically capable of it. I tried to weasel out. When I did, Catherine turned to me and spat: "Why aren't you strong like your mom?"

Catherine's insult shocked me at the time because I didn't know what she was talking about. My mother *wasn't* physically strong.

But, when I called up my sister recently to ask her, she told me that she did not realize my mother was ill when we were children—only later in the early '90s when we were in college. When I told her what Catherine had said to me, she replied, "Sure that makes sense. I think everyone thought of her as active and healthy." She reminded me that my mother had been athletic in her youth and she'd taken up tennis in her late thirties and forties. She played doubles tennis on a neighborhood court. She loved to garden—a labor-intensive endeavor that included shoveling and lifting. My mother also designed a tree house— a four-wall cabin, eight feet by ten feet, on stilts. My parents bought the lumber from a hardware store and did all the carpentry and construction by hand. The tree house lasted over fifteen years before being swept away in a flood.

I want to know how we could have had such divergent impressions of my mother's illness. Had I been so consumed by my fear that I misperceived my mother entirely? Because I was small and vulnerable, had I seen that in her as well? I'm sure of my memory of the symptoms, and both my sisters remember them too. But I'm the one that pieced them together to cast my mother as perpetually ailing.

vii.

In his editorial "Did Lady Windermere Have Cystic Fybrosis?" Bruce K. Rubin, MD, notes the connection between the syndrome and patients with cystic fibrosis. The inability to produce an effective cough results, most likely, from a gene mutation rather than an inherent desire to remain ladylike. He goes on to gently rebuke the medical researchers. "It has become a cottage industry to diagnose 'modern' diseases in historical figures who had unusual deaths, chronic illness, or physiognomy consistent with specific conditions. On the basis of extremely postmortem evaluations, Abraham Lincoln has been thought to have had Marfan syndrome, and . . . the Polish-French composer, Frederick Chopin, may have had CF. Although, the diagnosis of chronic illness in the long dead is an interesting blend of medicine and history, diagnosing disease in fictional characters falls under the realm of creative imagination."

The naming of a disease has serious implications for its diagnosis and treatment (just think "gay-related immune deficiency"). The name *Lady Windermere syndrome* appears to dismiss the truly terrible symptoms, ignores the syndrome's true form—one that it is debilitating, one that kills. It also genders the disease and in doing so genders its perception—it not only affects women but also women of a certain class, which seems entirely improbable. Rubin notes that despite the name and the social reproof implied by it, men should be tested and treated for Lady Windermere's syndrome. Precisely because of the name, it is possibly harder for a doctor to imagine a man suffering from it.

viii.

A librarian, Emma Watts, first writes *Chest* a letter noting that the character Lady Windermere isn't ill. She's a young bride with a small child—vibrant and not even, as Watts notes, particularly prissy. Watts is right. *Lady Windermere's Fan* is concerned with subverting and mocking social fastidiousness. Lady Windermere considers running away with the dissolute Lord Darlington because she believes her husband is cheating on her. Lady Windermere allows another woman to ruin her own reputation to preserve the very marriage she had just moments before considered turning her back on. Lady Erlynne, the woman so willing to sacrifice her reputation to protect Lady Windermere, is revealed to be blackmailing Lord Windermere by threatening to expose the truth of his wife's parentage. She is really Lady Windermere's mother.

Lady Windermere's Fan is meant to be a subversive play, up to a point. Wilde, unlike his contemporaries Ibsen and Shaw, is unwilling to explore the social conventions that trap women.

His Lady Windermere and Lady Erlynne are meant to tweak the scruples of high society, expose the moral hypocrisy that so angers Wilde.

It's this same anger that leads Wilde to sue the Marquess of Queensberry for libel. He misjudges his friends and believes the popularity generated by *Lady Windermere's Fan* and his later plays will protect him. After his release from prison, Wilde is shunned by the very society that once esteemed him and spends the rest of his life itinerant, nearly friendless, and in poverty. Reading about his last years is painful; to see a man whose life had been a brilliant, bravura performance, in all the best ways, reduced and humiliated is dispiriting. He is, in every account, broken and vulnerable. Even the famous last words—the witticism about the wallpaper—aren't in actuality his last words (the quip was uttered weeks before his death). At the end of his life, he asked for a Catholic priest in order to convert: "The artistic side of the Church and the fragrance of its teaching would have cured my degeneracies."

Richard Ellmann, in his biography of Wilde, contends more than once that Wilde died of complications from syphilis. But there exists no actual diagnosis of syphilis and this is the sort of extremely retrospective postmortem that Dr. Rubin criticizes in his article on Lady Windermere syndrome. This claim seems to share the same root as the insinuations about the green carnations: our fascination with the image of Wilde as having led a debauched life. We do know a few weeks before his death Wilde had surgery done on a painful abscess in his eardrum, the possible result of a bad fall he took while imprisoned. It is just as likely that a secondary infection from that surgery killed him. But now I'm conjecturing as well. We perceive whatever details allow us to make a palatable narrative of another person's suffering—that story a talisman against the overwhelming darkness of another's pain.

ix.

In my mother's wedding photographs, she appears dangerously underweight. My father told me that a cousin of his asked why he wanted to marry such a thin, frail woman. "You'll be taking care of her. She won't be caring for you." The first indication something was medically wrong, he said, had come when she applied for a visa to immigrate to England. Her lungs were so badly scarred my father and another family friend felt sure that the British immigration service would think she was very ill and turn down her application. The doctors, and my parents, eventually dismissed the scarring as the result of a childhood illness, and the event didn't come up again until I told my father what Dr. Kussin had said to us. My mother suffered her whole life—severe dry skin, suppressed appetite, shortness of breath, and, in her last two decades, muscle weakness, heart failure, and extended bouts of coughing. Before her diagnosis, we all had our ideas about what was wrong with her. As a teenager, probably after reading a Judy Blume novel, I determined that my mother was anorexic. For all our conjecture, none of us were ever right, and, more importantly, not one of us offered my mother any relief.

After my mother's death, my father said that my mother's deepest flaw was that she lacked optimism. She always expected the worst, he mused. It's true. She always worried and fretted. Sometimes I wonder if her pessimism was actually another symptom—a manifestation of the oxygen deprivation or an extension of the constant pain. We tend to think of illness as an add-on to a person—a tumor, an exposure to a viral infection. In my mother's case, so much of who she was and what she could accomplish stemmed from and came funneled through her lifelong struggle. It's impossible to separate the two.

X.

My mother was, technically, healthy when the nurse removed the CPAP. The machine had brought the level of oxygen in her blood to nearly normal levels. She was lucid and, even if she didn't feel any physical pain, knew what was happening to her. She was very afraid.

My mother, as she drifted to sleep, began to utter random sentences. She spoke mostly nonsense. At one point, she signaled to me to come near. She put her fingers on my arm. Her touch felt gritty and course against my skin. I noticed that her lips had started to take on a bluish tint, a sign of oxygen deprivation. "Tell my story," she said to me. "But start with the end."

"Why the end?" my sister whispered, her breath catching. I guessed, with a sorrow that nearly blinded me, what my sister was thinking. My mother wanted me to start with her choice to die.

"Because in the end," my mother replied, matter-of-factly, as if she was providing the most natural, obvious answer. "In the end, I survived."

In the Presence of God
I Make This Vow

1

The immigration lawyer informs me she is considering dropping my father and his new wife, Anoma, as clients.

"This looks like fraud," she says over the phone. She's talking about a package of materials that I've sent her meant to prove that my father and Anoma are truly married to each other. The lawyer must submit the materials to the Unites States Citizenship and Immigration Services so that Anoma can gain permanent status in the States and the right to apply for American citizenship. The process is ordinary—any noncitizen who marries a citizen must go through it—and really requires only the public display of a marriage that we as a society tend to expect. The problem is that no one—other than my father, Anoma, and two of her sisters—were aware until recently of the marriage.

My voice quavers. "It's not fraud. I really believe that."

I don't want the lawyer to refuse to represent my father and his wife, but I'm angry that I'm the one on the phone trying to help them. I myself didn't know, for a fact, about the marriage until a few weeks before my conversation with the lawyer and became aware of the possibility only a few months after my father had a severe, life-threatening stroke that left him disabled. It had humiliated me to put the package together at all—a nearly three-year history of a marriage I didn't know existed—and now I'm convinced the lawyer is mistaking my ambivalence for prevarication.

Bile surges into my throat, and I experience disgust at the sour, tangy aftertaste. I consider accepting the lawyer's attempt as an out, a way of my being free from having to help my father and telling my family that Anoma should make plans to leave.

The only noise is the steady, watery whoosh of traffic passing just beyond my curtained window. I stare at the empty, white wall in front of me. I've been a temporary tenant in my apartment for a year now, and I still haven't put art on the walls. I notice for the first time the paint isn't really white but stippled gray and uneven in places—more like the surface of a stone. The texture is mesmerizing and helps to focus me on my family's present need.

"I don't think it's fraud," I repeat, willing myself to sound more enthusiastic. "I believe they are genuinely married to each other." And this much is true. Whatever my anger toward them, I don't doubt *this* for a second.

"I recognize that every marriage has its own dynamic," the lawyer insists, "but there's so little here. There are no birthday cards. Not many photographs. He hasn't changed his will." It doesn't help that when the lawyer speaks she sounds weary, more than angry, and disappointed in my family as if she'd expected us all along to let her down. I know what she's implying. She thinks I'm part of whatever fraud she suspects because I'm the one that put the package of materials together. I'm reduced to yet another immigrant huckster trying to play the system.

She breathes deeply. "You're claiming that he isn't physically capable of traveling to DC, but he's traveling to Sri Lanka in four months." I blink at this. We wanted to spare him a trip to Washington, DC, to be interrogated by USCIS because he doesn't leave the house much. The trip to Sri Lanka is different. It's a family trip—we are all going—in part to help my father visit his homeland for the last time—the last time before he dies. His doctors have told him he shouldn't go, but he'd rather die there than not return to Sri Lanka one last time. Not one of us thinks this trip is going to be easy or particularly fun.

I also understand in that moment that the lawyer is vocalizing only what others—people trained to suss out con men and cheaters—will perceive. I sigh and parrot back her own words: *Every marriage has its own dynamic.*

"Well, here's the thing." Her tone has become hard. She wants to end this conversation, rid herself of a troublesome client. "It looks like he married her so that he could bring her over to work as his maid."

I feel the rush of blood to my face, the desire to ward away a deep humiliation. "My father has money," I say slowly, carefully. I, too, am growing tired of this conversation, and if she wants to stop helping us, she needs to say this directly. "He doesn't have to bring a maid from Sri Lanka. He could afford someone here."

Which is the real irony here because that's what he originally had told us she was. When Anoma first arrived, he'd lied and said she was working for him as a caretaker and that she was here on a temporary visa. That was also the reason I believed the marriage was real now. It seemed entirely natural, in retrospect, that a year after his wife's death, my father would find it hard to admit he had an emotional and physical need. He resorted to what he understood: an elaborate display of status.

When she still doesn't respond, I say, "I don't know why he kept his marriage a secret from us, but I don't think it was fraud." Then I add, 'It's cultural." The lawyer seems to accept this last statement at face value, though I feel terrible. I don't know any other Sri Lankans who would do what my father has done: marry his wife's cousin, bring her back to the States, and then lie to his three daughters and to both families. My father is a singular construct in that way.

2

In June 1592, Maria Audley, an attractive sixteen-year-old, maid of honor to Queen Elizabeth, met for the first time Thomas Thynne, the son of a politically prominent and wealthy Wiltshire landowner. Thomas, also sixteen, was studying at Oxford, but John Marvin, another prominent landowner and friend of the Thynne family, had asked him—some will say later lured him—back to Wiltshire for a short respite from his studies and, apparently, the opportunity to carouse. In other words, he'd been invited to party, and the seed that this was some sort of celebration had been planted in Thomas's head. In the historical records, Thomas Thynne is described as dark- haired and good looking, and his charm—which seems to be of the always-game-to-have-fun sort—is often noted. According to the accounts that exist, Maria was equally lively, doe-eyed, with strikingly dark, red hair. Chroniclers of this affair always note her hair; the detail becomes important later.

Thomas's parents did not accompany him, which isn't all that surprising given his age and stature. Maria's family—Lady and Lord Audley and her sister Amy—do accompany her. Maria, as a maid attending to Queen Elizabeth's most private needs, dressing her in the morning and undressing her at night, held a privileged position. The Queen's sovereignty was absolute. She was anointed by God. Maria would have received the honor of serving the Queen as part of a political favor. As might be expected, Queen Elizabeth carefully controlled the lives of those serving in her privy chamber down to the smallest detail. She even promised all her maids an arranged marriage to suitable men in possession of manners, political standing, and wealth. According to one account I found, the Queen so carefully monitored her courtiers' lives that she, at first, wouldn't let Maria leave her service even for a day. She eventually reluctantly agreed only after Maria's entreaties.

The weather in Wiltshire in the month of June would have been mild and most likely wet, but it was also the height of summer and could have easily been pleasant—the sort of romantic English pastoral you see re-created in film adaptations of Jane Austen novels. I like to imagine the breeze smelling wet and green, of gooseberries and of pine (mainly because that is my childhood memory of England). Thomas, a young boy easy to make happy, would have been buoyed by his return to this familiar countryside and the land that he loved.

He and his entourage didn't meet John Marvin at his estate but at a nearby inn—the Bell Inn. There he and his traveling companions would have most likely sat down at a banquet of trenchers, large, flat, stale bread used to hold meat and vegetables—and since there's a mention in the record of sweetmeats, there must have been several different types of meat with enough tryptophan to make even a grown man slightly groggy—and carafes of wine. At some point during this feast, Maria and the other women entered the room, and Thomas and Maria, despite the presence of both of their companions, sequestered themselves to a corner of the table. They huddled there for a long time alone, flirting and talking. According to one of the many depositions given later, the couple "grewe into such good liking each of the other as that they seemed desirous to be married presently."

That two sixteen-year-olds gorged on meat and, possibly tipsy, finding each other attractive seems entirely normal. What strikes me as curious is the reaction of Maria's parents, particularly her mother. Lady Audley appears to forget that her daughter serves the Queen of England and has been promised a very good marriage already. She also appears to forget that her daughter—at sixteen—is very young. According to later testimony—which may have been biased since there was a lot at stake for both parties—Lady Audley took her daughter's hand and twirled her around for Thomas. I can see Maria pirouetting, giddily, her farthingale lifting slightly to reveal tiny, slippered feet, the gold brocade of her dress sparking in the candlelight. She was, most likely, tiny, the size of a twelve-year-old now, but she also had to have been bold. Maybe it was her relationship to the Queen that gave her so much confidence. She must have learned early in her life that every action is a performance. Whatever the reason, it did not bother her to be displayed to a boy and did not bother her when her mother essentially, and I'm liberally translating here from the Old English, declared that if Thomas liked her face, he should see her body.

Someone in one of the entourages found a minister who had also stopped at the Bell that evening and asked him to marry the couple immediately. The minister is old, nearly blind, but he agreed. One of John Marvin's friends read the marriage ceremony out loud so that the minister, who couldn't make out the words himself, could repeat the important oaths. That June evening, Thomas and Maria promised in front of the relatively small gathering at the inn to cherish each other through sickness and health. John Marvin would later claim that he tried to caution Thomas and Maria and counsel them not to be governed by the moment, but if he did really say this, the couple did not take his advice. After the ceremony, their entourages accompanied Thomas and Maria to a bedchamber where both lay down together on the bed, fully clothed, and kissed, in full view of the Marvin and Audley families—a custom not unusual for the time. Though they both would later claim that they spoke intimately, the marriage was not sexually consummated that evening.

Maria's marriage to Thomas is odd for many reasons. Though they were legally old enough to be married, they were very young for people of their social standing. The landed gentry, during this time, tended to marry in their mid-to-late twenties. Most marriages of that time were elaborate social rituals, requiring negotiation—how much dowry should be paid, for instance—and planning. Thomas Thynne's parents weren't even there to give their approval.

The two families—the Thynnes and the Audleys—also hated each other. They were the wealthiest landowners in the county of Wiltshire, and they warred with each other over control of local politics. If the Audleys had tried to approach the Thynnes to arrange a marriage, it's unlikely they would have approved. Both Maria and Thomas probably feared angering his father and mother. Maria, certainly, feared angering Queen Elizabeth. For that reason, and, perhaps, because the alcohol had worn off, Thomas and Maria, the Marvins, and the Audleys, agreed not to reveal their marriage publicly.

3

Two years after Anoma arrived, when I still didn't know she was married to my father, we—and by *we* I mean my father, sisters, Anoma, and I—traveled to DC for a wedding. We stayed in a hotel, and I shared a room with Anoma.

My mother had been dead only a year when Anoma moved into our house. I had met her in Sri Lanka a few times, but I wasn't especially close to her. The impression I had of her was that she was meek.

She is as thin as a whippet—starved almost. But she has large, expressive eyes and full lips and in certain moments, when she dresses up or wears makeup, becomes very pretty. At the time she moved to the States, she was sixty-five, too old to find steady employment in Sri Lanka (the retirement age there was fifty-five), so she did various chores for members of my family to earn money. She was a relative who could be trusted in a country where few people, outside of one's family, can be. She revealed to me once, the only real interaction I had ever had with her, that she had wanted to be a nurse, but her father had fallen ill. She had made the choice to care for him for nearly a decade. The truth was, I thought of her as sad.

At the hotel, because it was the first time that we really talked, I learned more about her life. She had, it turned out, had a career working as a caretaker and aid for two families overseas. She had lived in Dubai and in Singapore and had liked both families she had worked for. They had paid her well, and she had led a cosmopolitan life, traveling freely in both cities, and making friends among other Sri Lankans who were similarly employed. She has a sister living in America, and her biggest dream was to come to America herself. She was thrilled to have accomplished that.

She was an odd mix of experiences. She had lived internationally, in major, urban areas, but this was the first time she had stayed in a hotel. I remember her awe sitting in the café the next morning, staring at the menu. She wasn't sure how to read it, and she wasn't very sure of what to order. She was thrilled when she received her breakfast basket—a biscuit, croissant, and jam—and apologized when she couldn't finish it all.

After his stroke, my father needed someone to bathe him, help him to the bathroom, speak for him. Anoma became that person. Her English is poor, so I deal with the nurses and the doctors, the negotiating with hospitals and critical-care services, but I am repulsed and cowed by the actuality of illness. I remember one morning, when my father was feeling particularly stressed, I could barely bring myself to touch him. His skin was moist and parchment-paper thin, and the feel of it sickened me. Anoma, though, found a washcloth and wiped his head and face and then held his hand and spoke softly to him in Sinhala. Later, she helped him into the bathroom and stayed with him to clean him. The one time she hadn't been around, and I had to help him to the bathroom, I nearly vomited. I'm not sure my father would have survived the stroke without her.

My sisters and I discovered the truth of their marriage a few months after my father's stroke while working with his accountant. My father and Anoma filed their taxes jointly. I had offered that they probably filed jointly to make things easier. "There's no reason for them to file jointly," my sister, a financial officer for a not-for-profit, explained. "Unless they're married."

When I asked Anoma if she were married to my father, she told me no. We had returned from the hospital. We were both exhausted, operating on little sleep, and overwhelmed by the day-to-day shifts in my father's health. I wondered, as I spoke, if she understood my English, but I didn't know how to say what I needed to say in Sinhala. Anoma clutched her purse to her stomach and stared straight ahead. Her voice was firm. They were not married. The immigration lawyer had helped her to get her visa. She even showed me her green card, which still had her maiden name on it. She had done nothing wrong. I asked her, then, if she really wanted to stay in America, if there was nothing here to keep her other than a work visa, and I was relieved when she replied, just as firmly as before, that she cared for my father, especially now that he needed her. Maybe I should have asked my father, but he seemed so often disoriented and so feeble I didn't want to upset him. Perhaps I should have pressed harder then, but the fact was my father and Anoma's marital status seemed to me to be the least of our problems. I wasn't sure my father was going to survive the hospital. I let it go.

4

I'm not someone to judge other people's marriages. I identify as bisexual, meaning, for me, that I'm open to, and have experienced a great deal of variation when it comes to sexual intimacy—a game-to-have-fun sort. I'm also introverted and private, and ambivalent when it comes to commitment. In my thirties, I had affairs with married men. The last affair I had was with the husband of a friend of mine. I thought he was physically attractive, and we connected because we were immigrants to the States and identified as such. He was open about his womanizing, and his wife, my close friend, was so sophisticated and knowing and beautiful (especially in comparison to me) that I thought she didn't care. I had no intention of breaking up their marriage. The sex was opportunistic—in his office or at my apartment—and had nothing to do with love. I never spoke to him on the phone. Whatever emotional intimacy we shared was sitting at the dining room table—the three of us— talking about loving country music as immigrants and our feelings of displacement and mutual loneliness.

One afternoon, I had stopped by their apartment in Midtown Manhattan to have lunch with her. We sat at the table sharing our meal, their one-year-old son between us. He giggled and gurgled and threw his food on the floor so that one of us would have to bend over to pick it up. If we refused, he'd grow agitated until we did what he wanted. "So needy. Just like his father," my friend had quipped.

She was beautiful—even in sweats and an oversized shirt, her hair pulled up and secured at the nape of her neck with a clip—and so sure of herself. I really loved her. I wanted to *hold* her. In her grace and warmth, she reminded me of my mother. I teased her, flirted a bit. I made gentle fun of her cooking. She had cooked the rice Persian style—so that it had crisped at the bottom and turned biscuit-like. I joked that in Sri Lanka we would have thrown that rice out.

I glanced over at the bookshelf—works in English and Farsi, books that belonged to both him and her, books that were shared, read together at the dining table, together in bed. It came to me in that moment that their apartment wasn't a place, but a living, breathing organism, each cell composed of the weaving together of the DNA of a marriage. The marriage was actual and palpable. I wasn't a friend, a lover, a mistress. I certainly didn't need to worry about being a threat. What I was was a short segment on a much longer strand. I remember being both awed by it all and recoiling briefly, not because of the affair, which was meaningless to each of us, but by the recognition that I'd been momentarily cannibalized. I was part of their relationship, and I served some purpose—something Old World and ancient. But we would never be truly able to acknowledge what that purpose was or that there might be some beauty in it. In another time, in another culture, but not in America, in that moment. Because of that, neither one of us could truly help the other. Because of that, I needed to go.

5

Thomas and Maria's marriage became public nearly three years after it took place. When Lord and Lady Thynne found out, they were devastated—and furious. For Lady Thynne it must have been a reproof, not only of her social standing, but her abilities as a mother. "How hard is my hap," she is said to have declared, "to live to see my chiefest hope and joy my greatest grief and sorrow."

Lord and Lady Thynne decided to pretend the marriage never took place and refused to acknowledge Maria or let

Thomas go to her. For them, the marriage represented the deepest of insults. There was, first of all, the issue of the dowry. They lost a substantial sum, approximately £1,500. There was the social stigma of not having been able to control a roguish son. And there existed the ever-deepening hatred they felt for the Audley family. The fact that they had not given consent, that Thomas was not living with his wife, and that the marriage had never been consummated was enough, in their eyes, to make the marriage invalid.

Maria lost the most from the public revelation of their secret marriage. The Queen dismissed her after the marriage was revealed. The Audley family later claimed that there existed a suitor—one picked out by the Queen—who was wealthier and far more stable than the young, charming Thomas. If Thomas died, before the validity of the marriage was legally affirmed, Maria would have no rights as his widow—including the right to inherit money or property. During the many years that the Thynnes refused to acknowledge the marriage, Maria existed suspended. As a woman already married, no other man would want her, but as a woman whose marriage wasn't recognized, she couldn't see, much less live, with her husband. There must have been a great deal of shaming directed at her.

When it was clear the Thynne family never planned to recognize her, Maria, aided by her family, brought her case to an ecclesiastic court. After the Thynne family learned of the impending court case, they launched their own lawsuit. The case lasted nearly four years, and most of the individuals present at the Bell that evening were deposed. Halfway through the trial, the minister died, a fact that Lord and Lady Thynne used in their favor. They submitted to the court accusations the now deceased minister had no standing to conduct a marriage because he had been convicted of stealing and adultery and that there existed a written covenant between him and the devil. When it looked like Maria might win her case, the Thynne family submitted accusations to the court, accusing the Audleys and their supporters of fornication and adultery.

Through all this, Lord Thynne didn't trust his son, Thomas, to say openly in court that he hadn't intended to marry Maria. Thomas expressed a deep fondness for Maria privately and publicly and a desire to remain married to her even though by now he had not seen her in person for a few years. When he was finally compelled to testify, enough social pressure had been placed on him that he acquiesced to his family's demands and stated that he had been duped into meeting Maria and had been too drunk to fully consent.

The story, though, does have something like a happy ending. The judge in the case eventually decided to speak to Thomas and Maria privately. Afterward, he determined that Thomas's testimony was influenced by his desire to please his parents, and that the young couple had both intended to marry and desired to stay married. Intention was all that was necessary. The marriage was valid.

After everything, Maria still tried to win her mother-in-law over, writing her several letters:

> To you my dearly loved mother are these lines sent from her that hath vowed to make herself as worthy as her best service can make her, of so kind a mother as yourself. . . . I crave nothing but your good opinion, which I will be thankful for.

In one of the letters she enclosed a lock of her red hair. It is thought that she did that to make herself real and palpable to a woman who still refused to meet her in person. Thomas and Maria Thynne never lived at his own estate during their marriage.

What evidence I've been able to find of Thomas indicates that he prospered in the years after the debacle. He remained wealthy and politically prominent, even serving in the House of Commons. Maria died in 1611, ten years after the judge validated her marriage, while giving birth to her third child. She was thirty-five.

The scandal surrounding the secret marriage and the court case consumed Elizabethan society. It was possibly, probably, an inspiration for *Romeo and Juliet,* though Shakespeare changed the setting to Verona and gives the romance between the two young lovers a much darker end. It also had an impact on the public perception of marriage at the time. Intention mattered. That a marriage was only just barely sanctioned and never consummated did not.

This perception of marriage as a private affair, one that could be simply witnessed by a clergyman, changed permanently 150 years later in 1753 with the passage of An Act for the Better Preventing of Clandestine Marriage, also known as the Hardwicke's Marriage Act. The bill rendered into statutory law what had long been ecclesiastical law: that in order for a marriage to be valid there had to be a formal, public ceremony and a banns or marriage license. It was not enough that a minister witnessed the exchange of vows. There needed to exist a formal, publicly witnessed ceremony, and the marriage had to be sexually consummated.

The bill's existence was pragmatic. It was meant to protect members of the upper class from being lured into hasty marriages by their social inferiors, and it was meant to protect wealthy men's property and ensure its strict transfer from people of wealth and social standing to other people of equal wealth and social standing. The law's actual effect, though, was to reify the idea that marriage is a public spectacle. Anyone who has had to endure two years of cake tastings, dress fittings, venue shopping, and in-law cat-fighting, while all the while wondering why she can't simply elope, has only to turn to the 1753 bill to locate the historical source of her misery.

I like to think of myself as someone who continually questions truths, but I've never really, until I started researching this, questioned marriage as pageant. In the Aughts, at the height of the fight for gay marriage, a friend asked if I'd changed my mind about getting married myself, and I told her I still fundamentally believed that the institution of marriage was problematic even as I defended tooth and nail LGBTQ rights. What I never wondered about was the whole open display of it—why we even needed it to celebrate a couple at all. Why we needed a wedding to buy presents, help furnish a home.

This insistence that marriage be a display—recognized legally and most cases by a religious institution as well—is powerful and renders so many important, perhaps equally important and necessary relationships socially and sexually deviant. Morganatic marriage. Mistresses (and whatever the male version of that is). Dominatrices. Polyamory. Companionate relationships that don't include sex. Military contract marriages. Queer marriages that have historically remained secret and private out of fear of the social and legal repercussions. When I ponder this list, which is probably very incomplete, partly because so many of these relationships have been lost to history, it seems strange to me how suspicious we are as a culture of any intimate relationship that doesn't look to us, well, like the state of being *married.*

6

My father's caretaker was the one who forwarded us the e-mail from the immigration lawyer. The three-year grace period had passed, and Anoma and my father now needed to prove that they were married in order for Anoma to remain in the country. The e-mail contained a list of documents Anoma and my father needed to supply: tax returns, photographs, birthday cards, testimony from relatives and friends, airline tickets, car and life insurance forms, a will. It was only then that we learned the truth. My father had married Anoma three years before in Sri Lanka.

Anoma and I sat in the kitchen, and she confessed to me that she loved my father deeply. She had not revealed the marriage when I first asked out of loyalty to him, because he was too ill to give her his approval to reveal the secret. As I spoke to her and realized how much she cared for him, I thought I could come to accept their relationship. Then she showed me a picture of her taken on her wedding day. Her hair is pulled back into a bun, and she is wearing makeup. She radiates pleasure, as does my father. At the physical presence of it, a secret picture from three years ago, I experienced a moment of head-spinning rage, something akin to what Lady Thynne must have felt long ago: I didn't know *anyone* at all.

I can't say why he didn't tell us and why he swore Anoma to secrecy. My guess is that he was embarrassed and afraid we'd be angry that he married a year after our mother's death. As time passed, it became harder to justify not revealing the truth earlier. I'm never going to get an answer from him, but, now, after some time, I've also come to realize, whatever my personal feelings, whatever my social expectations, my father and Anoma's marriage isn't really my business.

I have friends whose spouses are foreign citizens and whose marriages have been placed into limbo because of USCIS. One friend, a freelance artist, doesn't make enough money to prove to the government he can support his family. Even though he and his wife have a child, she can't apply for permanent residency. His wife travels between her native country and America, spending months away from her husband. Recently, the wife of the Indian engineer who was murdered in a Kansas bar lost her right to remain in the United States even though she has legal employment here. A congressman stepped in at the last minute to keep her from being deported. I think of Anoma. If my father were to pass away tomorrow, she would lose legal standing and have to return to Sri Lanka. Her dream to come to live in the States wouldn't matter. It doesn't matter how much love she or my father actually feel for each other. And through it all, I wonder what real business it is of anyone's. I wonder how much happier and secure so many people would feel, inside and outside of the institution of marriage, if we didn't insist so firmly on the rigid public moral spectacle of it all. I side with the judge in 1601 sitting listening to two twenty-something-year-olds declare their eternal, youthful adoration for each other. Who was he—really, who am I—to question the private nature of someone's love?

Pretty Girl Murdered

I'm waiting in Aunty's sitting room for lunch to be served. A heat wave is roiling through the Colombo streets, and, since I've arrived in Sri Lanka only a few days ago, every greeting and goodbye is punctuated by a condolence, "*Annay,* darling, you must be having so much trouble getting used to this weather." Suddenly, the color bleeds from the sky and the rain showers arrive. It's early July and still monsoon season. My aunt mentions how welcome the rain is, but for me, a visitor on a long holiday, the humidity only intensifies the stink of the city—diesel, human sweat, and rotting fruit. My skin feels as if it is dissolving in the wet air.

I nurse a glass of passion fruit cordial so syrupy my teeth ache with every sip; Aunty hands me the newspaper. She has carefully folded the front page to highlight the article, a detailed account of the week's local scandal, the murder of a 19-year-old club-hopping socialite. A large color photograph of the victim taken only a few weeks before her death accompanies the piece; she is attractive, fresh-faced, of indeterminate ethnicity. "Pretty Girl Murdered" reads the headline. "What if she was ugly?" I ask. My aunt has turned away to arrange the fall of her sari. She smiles coyly: maybe they wouldn't have bothered with the story at all. My aunt is joking and the victim's attractiveness aside, there are enough sensational aspects to make the story newsworthy. The murder—as sad and brutal as it is—also offers a distraction from the other front-page news items: the refusal of the prime minister to call elections and the government's failure to respond to the destruction caused by the Boxing Day tsunami. The headline with its qualifier is a declamation, a wistful acknowledgement, of a loss—in the midst of corruption—of something pure, innocent, refined.

I didn't grow up in Sri Lanka. My parents left when I was young and immigrated, eventually, to Rocky Mount, North Carolina. Sometimes I worry my reactions to Sri Lankan culture are too deeply colored by my upbringing in the United States. But my reaction to the headline "Pretty Girl Murdered" is not mere political correctness or exasperation with the country's journalism—though perhaps both play a part. To spend time in Sri Lankan middle- or upper-class society is to hear the idealized feminine often described as pretty, sweet, lovely, or hari shoke, a Sinhala expression roughly translated as very good, very cute, or pleasing. (The term can also describe a pretty object or a tasty cup of tea.) It's not unusual to see in Colombo's social pages headlines referring to the accomplishments and travails of "Pretty Girls." A quick perusal of personal ads seeking marriage partners finds demand for an "educated pretty girl," a plea from one mother to another for a "pretty daughter" for her son, and one ad for an "assertive pretty girl." Perhaps I'm surprised to see the colloquialism isolated in this context—the front page of a respected daily. Or maybe I simply realize that, while I've long accepted pretty girl without question, I don't know what it means.

Pretty girl does depend on physical attractiveness but not in the sense of a physical ideal; it doesn't have any sexual connotations. In fact, an overt display of sexuality would not be described as pretty. Truth is, I find *pretty* as hard to define as the nearly untranslatable Pali word dukkha, which describes the fundamental state of our existence.

I do know that the question I asked my aunt is disingenuous: the opposite of pretty isn't ugly. The pretty girl embodies a feminine ideal of proportion, coupled with strength of character. It's similar to the way society women in the novels of Jane Austen and George Eliot are described. In this sense, pretty girl has a musty, antique smell, a smell not entirely unpleasant but one that reminds me of times long faded.

I press myself against the back seat of the three-wheeler as it dodges traffic in the Fort. To distract myself from the numerous near misses, I stare out at the professional women—the bank managers, government officials, shop clerks—sporting saris, wrapped and draped in what is called here the "Indian style." No one struggles, as I do, to keep the fall from dropping from her shoulder in an inelegant puddle around her feet. Not one, I'm sure, secures the pleats with elastic tied around the waist as I have to. I am reminded of another aunty, one who, a few days before, as we were all dressing for a dinner party, asked me to help drape her sari.

She is in her mid-eighties and weak, barely able to walk without the help of a cane; she cannot turn to check if the back of her sari covers her petticoat. I kneel at her feet tugging at the hem to ensure that it is the proper length from the floor. I am diligent, obsessive, wanting to spare my aunt the humiliation of being seen with her slip showing. She points to a small sewing kit and asks me to take some safety pins and secure the sari fall to her jacket. She watches me through the mirror; when I'm finished she informs me with pride she never before had to pin the fall of her sari. Now she is afraid if it slips she will not be able to adjust it. Another concession to age.

In the foyer of her house, there is a photograph of her as a young woman, in her late teens or early twenties. My aunt is tiny but strong. She attended Sri Lanka's finest girls' school, Ladies College, and she is accomplished. She plays piano, speaks and writes English well, and was in her youth a gifted tennis player (a sport she played wearing a sari!). She is superbly and admirably proper. I can imagine Ella Wilcox, if she had met my aunt, describing her in the same way she describes Mrs. de Mel. And my aunt's photograph reflects all this. She is standing, lithe and elegant; her face is turned away from the camera to accentuate her profile. But what I've always admired is the sari. That sari transforms; a merely attractive woman becomes beautiful. When I was a teenager, I wanted to have a photograph made like this one, a photograph that would make me seem like this aunt. But when the time came, my mother refused to let me wear a sari. She felt I would look too traditionally Sinhalese for Rocky Mount, a rural Southern town. And somehow the resulting photograph—me in my prom dress—is a feeble copy.

To this day, I imagine how I might have looked if I had been allowed to pose as I had wanted. It would have allowed me uniqueness, a way of being different from all the other teens—white hoop skirts, ruffled necklines, braces glinting—who came to Olan Mills Portrait Studio to commemorate the first important night of their lives. My ethnic tradition might have made me a little more glamorous. But I've gotten it wrong. The "Indian style" of sari is not the traditional way of wrapping a sari in Sri Lanka; it was imported to Sri Lanka in the early part of the 20th century. The traditional dress associated with Sri Lanka, the Kandyan sari, is regional. During colonialism the bourgeois across the country adopted Western dress. If my aunt had posed for the picture twenty years before she would have chosen Western-style dress, a hoop skirt with ruffled neckline. But, by the 1920s, the Sinhalese Buddhist national movement had begun to call on Sri Lankan women to stop wearing

Western style clothing and revert to what they deemed tradition. In a way, I suspect unconsciously, my aunt's photograph is a political statement. And my prom picture seems to curl at the corners a little, fade even more.

Sri Lanka is a multi-ethnic, multi-religious country, but at the end of the 19th century it was Sinhalese Buddhism that began to emerge as the dominant force in the development of a nationalist ideology. Ancient Buddhism was closely tied to Hinduism—the two religions still share shrines to this day—and folk traditions. Two Westerners, the founders of the Buddhist Theosophical Society, Colonel Henry Steel Olcott and Helena Blavatsky, provided impetus to the idea of a pure Buddhist religion. Before their arrival, a Buddhist and Hindu revivalist movement had begun, but it was mostly a temperance movement. Olcott decried the influence of Christianity on Sinhalese society and on Buddhism, and it was Olcott who created the Buddhist catechism, the first Buddhist text to be used in Buddhist schools.

Olcott and Blavatsky's most lasting influence, arguably, is on the leading figure of modern Buddhism, Anagarika Dharmapala. Dharmapala was a disciple of Olcott and Blavatsky and had contact throughout his life with other leaders of the Theosophical movement. Dharmapala also spent a significant amount of time in Europe and America. But despite, or perhaps because of, his ties to the West, Dharmapala became a chief proponent of a nationalism that he believed would serve as an antidote to Western imperialism.

Dharmapala claimed the Sinhalese were a pure and chosen race, decedents of Aryans from Northern India. Buddhism was a pure and noble religion, and, according to Dharmapala, Islam, Hinduism, and Christianity had perverted the pure and tolerant society instituted by the early Buddhists. To this day,

Dharmapala is a polarizing figure in contemporary Sri Lankan culture. Some scholars trace the roots of the brutal, two-decade civil war to his brand of virulent nationalism. Others consider him a national and spiritual hero.

Dharmapala had contact with American feminists during the time he studied in the West and was aware of the American and European feminist movements. He was a keen and savvy politician and, recognizing the need to accommodate the growing political and social clout of Sinhalese women, he envisioned a specific role for women within his Sinhalese Buddhist nationalist movement. According to Dharmapala, Buddhism exalted and revered women, and the Sinhalese Buddhist woman would play a central role in the reinstitution of a truly Buddhist society. This woman would be the standard bearer, the symbol of the new purified culture, but as long as she accepted a role untainted by Western notions of progress. This necessitated the Sinhalese Buddhist woman give up Western dress and Western ideologies and accept the reinstitution of tradition. As Dharmapala wrote in a letter quoted by Kumari Jayawardena in her book *Feminism and Nationalism in the Third World*:

> The Aryan husband trains his wife to take care of his parents, and attend on holy men, on his friends and relations. The glory of woman is in her chastity, in the performance of household duties and obedience to her husband. This is the Aryan ideal wife.

Dharmapala's claims of the purity and the primacy of Buddhism have had serious political consequences for Sri Lanka. The claims have also had serious consequences for the progress of feminism in the country. The nascent Sri Lankan feminist movement by the early 20th century subsumed its activism under the nationalist banner. This new nationalist movement through the provision of a few intermittent concessions—for example women's suffrage—was able to promote the illusion of progress while never truly addressing the fundamental inequities in the culture. And Sri Lankan women, with some notable exceptions, accepted that their strength and progress were embodied in the reestablishment of an ancient tradition, a tradition that was in large part an invention.

Colombo is an international city. Tourism is a major industry, and between the NGOs and the global corporations, there is a large community of foreign nationals. Sri Lankan women wear saris to work and change into Western-style clothing to go out for coffee in the evenings. Thirteen years ago, when I explained to my relatives I rented my own apartment and did not live with my parents, they found my independence disturbing. By 2006, more and more, women are buying homes and apartments and living alone. Young women don miniskirts and go to nightclubs. While newspaper editorialists bemoan decadent Western influence and lax moral standards, equal space is given to feminists who counter that women have the right to dress how they want without having their morals impugned. There exists also, as in India, a '60s-style sexual revolution, with women more and more open about their sexuality.

Unlike other parts of the third world, where gains in women's rights have led to backlash, Sri Lankan culture, while always insisting on the primacy of the pretty girl, has responded to the change with some tolerance. In fact, Sri Lanka has long promulgated, at home and to the world, a view of itself as among the least oppressive countries in the third world as regards women's rights. In 1960, Sri Lanka elected the world's first female prime minister, Sirimavo Bandaranaike. From 1994 until November 2005, Chandrika Bandaranaike Kumaratunga, a woman of notable strength and fortitude, served as prime minister. Sri Lanka has long allowed women to pursue professions and today has a large middle-class female workforce. Sri Lankan culture has no history of sati, dowry murders, and ritual seclusion; there is no ban on widow remarriage. Here, rape is punishable in a court of law.

Close examination, however, reveals deep contradictions. Sirimavo Bandaranaike was elected to office on a sympathy vote after the assassination of her husband. Chandrika Bandaranaike Kumaratunga is the scion of one of Sri Lanka's most prominent political dynasties—a sort of Sri Lankan version of a Kennedy. Women, especially poor and rural women, are still significantly underrepresented in the parliament and upper-level civil service positions. Middle-class women have made significant gains, but these gains have bypassed poor and rural women. There is still strong pressure on middle-class career women to marry and have families; when these women do have families, there is strong pressure for them to give up their careers. This is the irony of being a Sri Lankan woman: the dual role as a "pretty girl," a national ideal and the global symbol of women's progress in the third world.

When I speak to my strong-minded, strong-willed female relatives and friends, almost all of them acknowledge the pressures and the strictures of this coupling of traditional roles for women with a desire for feminist reform. They almost always bring up a popular contention that ancient Sinhalese culture was, in part, matriarchal. It was colonialism that institutionalized patriarchy. This is offered in part as proof that strength is ingrained into the Sinhalese woman's identity.

According to this version of history, in pre-colonial Sri Lanka, there existed for women two forms of marriage, diga or binna. If a woman entered in a diga marriage, she went to live with her husband. If she entered in a binna marriage, the husband came to live in the woman's home. A binna marriage allowed for the woman to inherit her father's property and to expel her husband, at any time, if she so chose. My friends also like to gleefully point out, there also existed instances of women exercising their sexual freedom by engaging in fraternal polyandry.

The British colonial regime was scandalized by the reports of polyandry and binna marriage. While they were not wholly successful in ending certain practices—the colonial administration did grant divorces if both the wife and husband consented—they were able to institute marriage and inheritance laws that favored the husband.

This history is very popular, especially among young women. Written versions appear on the Internet and in scholarly articles. But when I go in search of the actual sources, I find the reality to be more complicated. Women did not have the right to choose the form of marriage contract they entered but were given in diga and binna marriages by their fathers. The wife's home in a binna marriage was the wife's *father's* home. Binna marriages were in reality utilized to ensure heirs for the father's property, and women who left their binna marriages and then entered into a diga marriage lost any right to inheritance.

And as for the polyandry, studies done by the anthropologist S. J. Tambiah note that it was either a means of consolidating resources in times of extreme poverty or an extreme reaction to the possibility of cuckoldry. Either way, the brothers (or in some rare cases several distantly related men) chose to share their wife. Another anthropologist notes the records of the British colonial administration accounts for only sixty-one instances of polyandry. Hardly a case for sexual freedom in pre-colonial Sri Lanka. Still, even if it's not entirely true, there is something compelling about the need to find, within history, a strong, independent image, an antidote to the pretty girl.

But the pretty girl, herself, is a contrivance. She belongs to a history I have heard all my life: Sinhalese women, because of the influence of Buddhism, had during the pre-colonial period a degree of freedom that outside forces took away, and that it is Buddhism, an inherently tolerant religion, that allows women's freedom today. But I now know this is myth developed and propagated as central to a Buddhist (and eventually to a national) identity.

At lunch, a few weeks later, my aunt hands me a copy of an interview I'd given to a Colombo newspaper dedicated to women's fashion and lifestyle. I'd shown up for the photo shoot in jeans and blouse, no makeup. But the photograph in the paper is doctored. I'm wearing bright red lipstick. The editors of the paper have attempted to give me the veneer of a pretty girl. When my aunt points this out, I laugh. Truthfully, I find the doctored photograph a bit off-putting. It points to a failure on my part. I take the paper from my aunt, fold it so that the photograph is covered, and tuck it away so no one else can see.

Confessions of a
Dark Tourist

I realized at some point during lunch that the house we—the
two Sri Lanka Security Forces soldiers, my cousin, my friends,
and I—occupied was once someone's home. The house, itself,
resembled a thousand others like it in Sri Lanka: one story with
a slate roof and a verandah that led into a small sitting room.
Any traces of the person or people who had once lived there
had been erased. The cheap, plastic furniture had been positioned haphazardly around the room with little attention to
design or comfort. The clay floors were scuffed and badly in
need of repainting. A doorway on the far side of the room led
into a long hallway at the end of which I could make out silhouetted forms scuttling back and forth, all head and limbs like
shadow puppets. The heat, the slick, liquid air that wilted my
hair and my clothes, the soldiers, the foreignness of this area
of the country I had never before visited had already made me
uncomfortable and uneasy. Now the realization that someone
very different from me once called this place home, and that
person was most likely dead, made me wish I had never come.

Both soldiers, majors in the army, sported camouflage uniform. Big men, broad and muscular, they exhibited an un-self-

conscious masculinity. One, darker-skinned and handsome, appeared more sympathetic than the other. He spoke intelligently and even at times seemed quite sad. It was easy, given the cultural and social gulf between us, to imagine him as some sort of philosopher-warrior. The other soldier, whose last name I remember as Dias, exuded an arrogance I found off-putting. My friends had told me not to say anything to the soldiers—I wasn't really supposed to be there—and one of the soldiers— Dias, the arrogant one—wanted to know why I was so quiet. "Don't you like the food?" he demanded. To prove that I did indeed like the food I hopped up to go serve myself seconds.

I entered a room that must have once been a dining room. The food was arranged buffet style, and I served myself a little bit of curry though I really wasn't that hungry. When I turned around, the other soldier, the one I found sympathetic, stood behind me. I jumped, and he seemed genuinely sorry for having surprised me. I hadn't expected to actually meet soldiers on this trip. I also hadn't expected to sympathize with them. I had read the reports of the atrocities committed during the war and built up, as a result, one image of the Sri Lanka military. The soldier asked me if I liked the meal, and I answered hoping that he didn't notice my heavily accented Sinhala. Because I didn't want him to ask any more questions, I scurried away.

The whole exchange had a farcical quality to it that I played up for laughs back at the hotel where my friends and I were staying. For a moment, as I pantomimed trying to communicate with the soldier, I believed it possible that what we were doing, what I was doing, wasn't quite as terrible as it felt.

In 2011, I participated in a war tour conducted by the Sri Lanka Army to Jaffna and Mullaitivu, former battle zones in the North of Sri Lanka. These war tours, led by the Security Forces branch of the Sri Lanka Army, are very common now and have been condemned by numerous human rights organizations, but when I was allowed to Jaffna and Mullaitivu in 2011 these tours had only begun.

My cousin and two of her closest friends work for one of Sri Lanka's largest banks, Commercial Bank of Ceylon. Through contacts in Jaffna and with the help of a security guard at their bank who had once served with the Sri Lanka Navy, they arranged for a tour of an area of the North that was restricted for most civilians and foreigners. For the trip, because I had renounced my Sri Lankan citizenship in order to become an American citizen, I had to apply for special clearance to travel, which entailed giving up my passport for a few days and providing a photograph. I received a letter granting me clearance to enter Jaffna but it did not cover all of the areas to which my cousin and her friends were visiting. My friends decided since I was part of a group of Sri Lankans—a group of Sinhalese—that I should accompany them anyway. My uncle advised me that if anyone questioned me to tell them, firmly, my last name was "Sirisena," a surname that identified me as ethnic Sinhalese.

Sinhalese Buddhists form the majority ethnic group in Sri Lanka, and we dominate the government, the military, and the police. Tamils make up a much smaller minority of the population of Sri Lanka as a whole, but they make up the majority in the northern regions of the country. After independence from England, the Sinhalese Buddhist majority disenfranchised the Tamil people and limited their participation in most spheres of life—civic, academic, cultural. In the early 1980s, the Liberation Tigers of Tamil Eelam, claiming to represent Tamil interests, began fighting successive Sri Lankan governments to establish a Tamil homeland in the North of Sri Lanka.

If you read enough accounts of war, you begin to notice that there's a point in every conflict when it seems it might go on interminably, become the forever war. And it certainly looked at one point as if the LTTE would never stop. By the early 2000s, after twenty years of fighting, the LTTE had nearly achieved regional autonomy in the North with an infrastructure it built and the ability to collect tolls along the A9 and issue speeding tickets. The LTTE also established a kind of cultural autonomy. The journalist Amy Waldman, in a January 2003 article in the *New York Times,* described traveling through the North: "A large billboard along the A-9 road, which runs through Tiger territory on its way north, shows women how to fully exploit their deaths. If wounded in battle, colorful graphics demonstrate, they are to play dead until enemy soldiers approach, and then blow up as many as possible—and themselves in the process." That the Sri Lanka Army did eventually destroy the LTTE was seen then as an enormous, once nearly unimaginable, victory by the Sinhalese majority.

Though Jaffna and Colombo are only 363 kilometers apart, roughly the distance between New York and Washington, DC, some Sinhalese in the south view Jaffna and its surrounding provinces as something exotic, almost foreign—different soil and vegetation, different food, different customs, different language. The division only deepened during the war. My mother, who is Sinhalese and Buddhist, visited Jaffna only once as a child. The cousin who arranged the current trip on which I was tagging along had traveled to Jaffna only one other time during the peace talks. Other members of my family—especially those born after the fighting began—have never traveled there. Jaffna holds an allure for many Sri Lankans—part of the country and, yet, separate.

I thought briefly of using the lack of a full permit to bow out. I had mixed feelings about going. Jaffna and the area surrounding it had experienced extraordinary brutality and I couldn't imagine that two years provided enough time for a recovery. I also worried about appearing to be among the conquerors come to survey the spoils. I hadn't yet heard the term dark tourism, but I did recognize that serious ethical and moral questions existed. I also knew I was never going to have a chance like this to see the actual scars of war. My experience of the war had been up to that point distant—reading about it in books and newspapers.

The night before we left, I tossed and turned under my mosquito net. I was already awake and dressed when my cousin knocked at my bedroom door at four-thirty. When we all piled into a van an hour later, Colombo rested, still quiet, the roads nearly empty. It had rained the night before and a fine, gray mist arced over the blackened tar. Slivers of early morning light winked from between the cornerstones of white stucco houses.

Despite not having received nearly enough sleep, an adrenaline rush buoyed me, the feeling that I was doing something truly daring. I carried with me a knapsack containing along with my clothes, sunglasses, a sunhat, a bottle of suntan lotion, bug spray, and packets of Munchee Chocolate Puffs. I had prepared as if I were going to the beach because truly what do you carry into a former warzone? My cousin, who had taken a seat in the front just behind the driver, kept my security clearance with her. If we ran into any problems with the soldiers, my uncle had designated her to speak for me.

Civil War battle site tourism, tourism to visit World War I and World War II battlefields, visits to Auschwitz all fall under the category of war tourism. In other words, visitors who never lived through the war—or most likely any war—pay money to go to a site and be accompanied by a tour guide—if at all possible a survivor able to provide a firsthand account. War tourism has a long history. Scholars John Lennon and Malcolm Foley, in a work published in 2000, accorded this type of tourism a more sinister appellation—dark tourism. Dark tourism is a broader category that includes tours to former sites of any type of catastrophe, natural or man-made. In *The Darker Side of*

Travel, Richard Sharpley and Philip R. Stone define dark tourism this way: "the act of travel to sites associated with death, suffering, and the seeming macabre." War tourists don't limit their travels to places in which conflict is a thing of the past. A destination tour website in the UK happily touts that tourism to Afghanistan has increased 100% and tourism to Iraqi Kurdistan, it appears, has increased by 70%.

The question is what attracts visitors to such sites. Sharpley and Stone offer a few reasons. Visitors may be drawn by "a simple morbid curiosity, through *schaudenfreude,* by a collective sense of identity or survival 'in the face of violent disruptions of collective life routines.'" Novelty, the desire to participate in your own adventure narrative, and nostalgia are also posited as potential reasons. A voyeuristic impulse is a motivator. Grief plays a role.

It's true that there's a huge divide between visiting Antietam on a Saturday afternoon and paying thousands of dollars to travel to Aleppo. But, according to Sharpley and Stone, what characterizes all war tourism is an emphasis on extreme otherness. The contrivances of Disney World and Las Vegas are designed for the tourist's comfort and enjoyment, but the dark tourist site promises an "authentic" brush with death, grief, mayhem, murder. And the experience promises to be transformative: the dark tourist goes from passive bystander and mere consumer of history to witness, with all the uniqueness and privilege that being a witness affords in this culture.

Expertly curated sites such as Auschwitz and Gettysburg National Military Park exist on the same continuum as the war tours conducted in the former Yugoslavia or in Sri Lanka. The dictum "Never Again" coexists uneasily with a thirst for the morbid. Perhaps the only true measure of how tasteful a war tourism site is, then, is the amount of time that has passed since the main event. Any tourist who trespasses that line too soon risks being haunted by a sense of their own rapaciousness. As Alfred Ely, one of the original Civil War dark tourists writes in his memoir, "Among other things, I found that to visit battle-fields as a mere pastime, or with the view of gratifying a panting curiosity, or for the sake of listening to the roar of shotted artillery, and the shrill music of flying shells (which motives however were not exactly mine) is neither a safe thing in itself, nor a justifiable use of the passion which Americans are said to possess for public spectacle."

My cousin and my friends have spent their entire lives in the middle of a war. They are either divorced or unmarried and none of them have children. In fact, of the whole group of friends only a handful is married. This gives them a lot of freedom to travel—they've traveled all over the world—and a great deal of disposable income. In the '90s, the government claimed that Sri Lanka's universities—many of them of very high quality and well-respected throughout the world—were hotbeds of political agitation and shut them down. Many college-aged students left the country to attend university overseas and, because of the political situation, never returned. It seems to me that men were more able to leave than women since women were expected to shoulder the burden of caring for their parents. These women who remained have done well—become bankers, lawyers, journalists, politicians. My cousin and my friends are successful, but you can hear in the way they speak a sense of loss, a sense of something important being missed, and occasionally of bitterness.

For most of the journey to the North of Sri Lanka the A9 was paved, but as we drew closer we hit rough patches—places where the road was heavily pitted or even parts that had never been properly paved. The government had recently committed itself to repairing the A9 as part of a massive development project in the North and had received most of its funding from

China. Part of the conditions of the funding—or so the news-papers reported—was that the government use Chinese work-ers. As we drove we saw tents shielding helmeted Chinese road workers from the sun as they sipped at teacups. Every thirty miles or so, we were stopped at a checkpoint or passed an army regiment bivouacked at a point in the distance. Any sense that the LTTE had ever patrolled the A9 had disappeared.

The landscape of northern Sri Lanka is very different from that of the southern region. Most of Sri Lanka is verdant, green, lush with jungle vegetation. But Jaffna appears vast and flat—all hard clay and limestone dotted by the tree that is the symbol of the region, the Palmyra, a tall palm with a thin trunk topped by a crest of palm fronds that make it look a little like a giant green and brown Q-tip. The houses are often painted bold shades—blue, pink, apricot, as if to defy the monotone earth tones of the surrounding terrain. Candy-striped stucco walls mark a Hindu shrine or temple. Sri Lankans in the South can be dismissive of the Jaffna landscape, refer to it as ugly. Whereas the landscapes of the South are jammed-packed with people, cars, animals, and billboards, the landscapes of the North ema-nate the rugged, off-putting barrenness we associate with des-erts. Leonard Woolf served as an administrator in Jaffna for several years. He wrote of Jaffna in his memoir *Growing*: "Here again is one of those featureless plains the beauty of which is only revealed to you after you have lived with it long enough to be absorbed into its melancholy solitude and immensity."

As we drew closer to Kilinochchi, once the seat of the LTTE, the yellow caution tape marked in English, Sinhala, and Tamil with the word MINE became ubiquitous. We passed at another point female villagers—deminers—decked out in white hel-mets and visors kneeling hunched forward so they could exam-ine the ground. (The CEO of one of the NGOs involved in demining operations in the North and Northeast informed me that the NGOs who recruit these women are very careful to ensure their safety. She was very proud of the fact that up to the point that I spoke to her, no civilian deminer had been killed.) The mood in the van shifted. We listened to ABBA and Eagles on the way, and we didn't stop the music, but my friends began to share their memories of the war. One friend recounted how during the university shutdowns she'd lied to her parents and snuck into movie theaters during the day. "I'd sit there and feel terrible," she admitted. "I thought, what if the theater was bombed and I was killed. My parents would know I had been going with boys."

When we arrived at our first stop, an army jeep drew up next to us, and soldiers hopped out. What I hadn't expected, and what makes the war tour I participated in Sri Lanka unusual, was that our tour was almost entirely coordinated by the Sri Lanka Army Security Forces headquartered in the area. Essentially, soldiers became our tour guides. Most were officers, though a few were infantrymen. My cousin and my friends decided that I shouldn't speak much—we didn't want to invite any inquiries into where I was from or have them ask for my papers—and that I shouldn't take notes, at least not during the tour itself. I resolved not to draw attention to myself. I can't say I wasn't frightened—we were dealing with soldiers after all— but it did seem to me that the soldiers were cowed by the presence of six affluent, well-dressed, women from Colombo. They were many of them garrulous, effusive with information, and shared at every moment possible insights into their lives during the war.

The sites that the soldiers escorted us to were caught in some halfway stage between what they had once been and a stop in an almost theme-park-like series of attractions. The army had, I was very surprised to see, erected signs in both English and Sinhala (but not Tamil). The signs were not written in the well-researched, semi-academic prose that you associate with markers at most historic sites. Instead the signs touted carefully worded propaganda meant to exalt the military and to remind the viewers—the Sri Lanka Armed Forces clearly expected the viewers to be mostly foreigners and Sinhalese—of the terrible deeds the LTTE committed. At a swimming pool used to train LTTE divers, the signage read: "While the nation was swarming with pools of blood with the spate of LTTE's heinous crimes elsewhere, the terrorist had constructed this huge swimming pool in 2001 for exclusive use of the cream of terrorists." Over two days, the Security Forces escorted us to bunkers used by LTTE leaders, a makeshift war museum exhibiting LTTE weaponry, an LTTE village, an LTTE junkyard, even restricted areas of Mullaitivu including Puthumathalan, which was the site of some of the heaviest fighting in the final days of the war.

At an LTTE prison, the soldiers led us to the empty prison cells. They told us this secret prison in the middle of the jungle was where the Tigers had held Sri Lanka Armed Forces soldiers and Tamils whom the Tigers considered traitors. The steel doors of most of the cells had been removed and the doorways, all placed at regular intervals, stood empty, six long slivers of darkness, stark against the egg-carton-gray prison walls. A large margosa tree arced over the building on one side. Behind the prison, a stretch of red clay dirt bloomed where the grass had begun to die away. A miasma of clay dust, kicked up by our van and the army jeeps that escorted us to the prison, hung in the air. The landscape shimmered behind it, slightly distorted, like objects viewed through a scrim. It was early afternoon, and the sun had begun to bear down, searing the skin on the back of my neck. Between the two buildings was a long trench now overgrown with grass. The soldiers told us that during heavy shelling the LTTE made the prisoners shelter inside the trenches.

The soldiers urged us to take pictures. One soldier gestured to me to follow him, and I did. He led me to a cell and demanded I step inside. The cell was narrow, barely four feet in width, and there was just enough room for me and another friend who had joined me when the soldier began to lead me away.

The soldier waited outside the cell as my friend and I entered. He yelled to us that most of the Tamils kept in the prison were Christian. This was only our first day of our war tour, but I already felt depressed, scared by the presence of so many soldiers, and overwhelmed. The cell was dark, except for a small window on the far end covered with bars. The outline of some sort of ledge was barely visible underneath. I didn't try to explore it. I was sorry to be standing there at all.

On the wall spread a chalk drawing of an enormous tree, the branches and leaves curving and intertwining together to form an intricate network of abstract shapes. There was also writing in Tamil that none of us, my friend, the soldier, or me, could read, and a series of numbers. My friend asked the soldier what the numbers meant. He shrugged because he either didn't know or didn't care. "It's a calendar," I replied.

The Sri Lanka Army's motives, at the time we arrived, might not have been entirely triumphal. General Sarath Fonseka, one of the architects of the campaign that had ended the civil war, had been arrested a few months before on charges of corruption. The feeling among the army was that the arrest was unjust and politically motivated—Sarath Fonseka had attempted to run against the president in 2009. Many of the officers and soldiers must have also been aware of some of the war crimes allegations being leveled against them by the Western press, Tamil journalists and politicians, and even some members of the Colombo elite. These war crimes allegations included bombings of civilian targets and genocidal rape.

One of the many stops on our war tour was the former LTTE leader Velupillai Prabhakaran's bunker. The soldiers ushered us into the first level—a spare room with a cot to one side. The mattress had been stripped bare and the fabric was stained brown with sweat and age. Over the bed hung a framed portrait of Prabhakaran in camouflage standing next to the LTTE flag. On a far wall rested a garment rack; a neatly pressed and folded combat uniform hung from one of the rungs. In the corner, on a cushioned bench, sat a large, stuffed toy cheetah. The walls had been painted a light blue, paint chips peeling from the wall. The room was lit with a single light bulb. The air tasted heavy on the tongue and faintly bitter. Whoever had designed this room had reconstituted it to resemble one of those "this-is-how-they-lived" displays you find in museums, with only the velvet rope barrier missing. But there existed a sparse—haphazard—feel to the whole creation that put me off a bit, as if a child had pieced it all together. My cousins and my friends walked around snapping pictures.

After we had spent ten minutes in what appeared to be Prabhakaran's bedroom the soldier led us down a rickety staircase to a bottom level. According to the soldiers, the entire bunker was multiple stories and included secret passageways that would provide Prabhakaran escape if necessary. The one level we were shown was dark, lit by a faint bulb strung from the ceiling. I couldn't see much of anything except that there appeared to be a lot of wood and metal on the ground. The concrete walls secreted an intestinal ooze that glistened in the half-light. By then I could barely follow the soldier's Sinhala and couldn't make out my cousin or any of my friends in the dark. A military engineer—a good friend of one of the women on the tour with me—had joined us, and he offered a few facts in English—dimensions and information of what the room had been used for originally. He called it a war room.

When we came back up, I noticed an object sitting on what I assumed was once Prabhakaran's bedside table. It was metal, the dimensions of a crock-pot. I asked my friend to ask a soldier what it was. He shook his head at her question. My friend offered that perhaps it was for developing film canisters, though that didn't seem right to me. I had studied photography in art school. I did know enough to recognize it was mostly likely some sort of centrifuge. In the van, I drew up a quick sketch of the object. When I returned to Colombo I determined, through some research on the Internet, what it really was—a centrifuge used for plasma separation. Prabhakaran, a diabetic, would have needed to be able to get accurate medical results if he spent a long time in the bunker. I don't know why but the centrifuge stays with me.

Alfred Ely, the dark tourist I quoted earlier, paid a steep price for his sense of adventure. He wandered too close to the fighting at Manassas and was discovered by Confederate soldiers. In his *Journal of Alfred Ely: A Prisoner of War in Richmond,* he writes about his capture in understated language that still makes clear how harrowing his experience must have been: "The officer . . . took me to the colonel, sitting on horseback, and introduced me in these words: 'Colonel, this is Mr. Ely, Representative in Congress from New York,' to which the colonel, in a most angry tone, replied, drawing his pistol, and pointing it directly at my head. . . ."

Ely was held for over five months in a Confederate prison in Richmond. By Ely's own account his captors treated him well. He did witness several acts of brutality—a soldier shooting at a prisoner for looking out a window and the long illness and eventual death of another civilian also taken prisoner at Manassas. He also became the butt of spectatorship himself. Southerners arrived at the prison in crowds to see, in person, the "Yankee prisoner." The most poignant parts of the journal for me are those places where he wrestles with his feelings about the war and the irony of his situation: "I am a prisoner of war, and that, too, in my own native land! Within these walls I am the victim of an unhappy civil discord in the nation of American freemen, the happiest, freest, and most prosperous people on earth." These words remind me of a terrible truth of civil war: how you can find yourself both citizen and insurgent.

Ely did, unlike me, go from war spectator to victim, and as a victim he was able to witness firsthand the toll of the war on the South. He dedicates the bulk of his memoir to a detailed account of day-to-day life within the prison and documenting the experiences of the other prisoners. Yet, Ely keeps asking himself throughout his memoir how he came to find himself in a Confederate jail. He returns continually to his own curiosity, which appears to him increasingly troublesome and inappropriate given the suffering he witnesses.

Ely's experiences are important to me because they truly were transformative. He became a witness and advocate for Union prisoners of war and wrote movingly and compassionately of individual members of the Confederacy. But here again it seems to come down to a matter of distance. Ely went from outsider to intimate when he was discovered transgressing the battle perimeter and that's what truly validates his journey. There remains the central question: if a war tour, in order to ensure a participant's safety and to maintain a sense of credibility and tastefulness, has to maintain such distance—temporal, proximate—what is the point?

One evening, colleagues of my cousin drove us to a remote beach in Jaffna for a picnic dinner in the moonlight. Our escorts were all Tamil and had lived in Jaffna for the entirety of the war. The beach was pristine, left largely untouched by humans. There aren't many pristine beaches left in Sri Lanka, but the civil war retarded economic development in Jaffna, especially along the beachfront, and as a result the local flora and fauna had been allowed to thrive. There were also a large number of wild dogs that prowled the perimeter of our picnic site. If we noticed their courage building and if they begin to act boldly, we threw pebbles at them to make sure they knew to keep away.

During our war tour, the Jaffna sun had shimmered above us, exuding a relentless heat, but by sunset the air had grown cooler. The sand, though, was still warm. I spread out my beach towel and buried my toes to enjoy the sensation of heat. The spray from the ocean coated us so that our skin, our hair, our clothes gleamed.

Our hosts set up, in a cabana, a camping stove. I picked up my beach towel and sat in the shelter with a friend and a group of Tamils—two men and a young woman with a child—that had accompanied the host. They spoke to each other in Tamil and one of the men spoke to my friend in Sinhala. As we started to eat, I raved to my friend in English about the food. I noticed the woman with the child smiling and realized she spoke English. I smiled at her and asked her a question directly. She laughed and in near-perfect English answered our questions and told us a bit more about herself. She had worked as an English teacher before she married.

The crab curry was so spicy my fingers, tongue, my sinuses burned, and my eyes watered. But I couldn't stop eating. Towards the end of our meal, as my friend and I shoveled bits of crabmeat into our mouths a young man seated across from us explained that just across the road, a few hundred yards from where we were seated, existed a mass grave. The LTTE had massacred perceived traitors there. I nodded solemnly at his story. I'd heard by then a lot of stories like his. The woman across from us shifted the baby in her arms, and adjusted the cloth the child was wrapped in. I wanted to talk to the woman more, and I tried to catch her eye. But she fussed over her baby and never looked in my direction again.

The beach had become completely, spookily dark. There was no illumination other than a few flashlights and the pinhole moon hovering above the horizon. My cousin and some of my friends decided to take a sea bath. I remained on the shore. Beside me, one of the hosts turned off his flashlight and nudged me. He whispered, "Look." In the seconds that I had turned away, the sea had transformed. The surface sizzled, thousands of brilliant, tiny sparks, like the sputtering of firecrackers. "Fish," my host exclaimed. Trillions of tiny bioluminescent fish. It came to me in that moment, staring at all that untouched beauty, an understanding that had until then eluded me. The war wasn't only a collection of horrors, a catalogue of crimes. The war with its continual churning destruction, its impeding of progress, had frozen us all in time, and that's what I had added to by joining this war tour, a sense that none of us would ever move on from this time and place.

On the afternoon of the last day of our Jaffna tour, the two officers we had dined with the first day arranged for a small, parting lunch. Dias and his more sympathetic colleague arrived to the breakfast no longer in uniform but sporting instead neatly pressed khakis and polo shirts. They appeared at ease and joked and teased us a bit. We all sat laughing and chatting over plates of idiyappam and kiri hodi. A friend of mine joked with the officers, "Is this how you ate on the battlefield?" Dias guffawed, "No, not at all. We ate from packets." He pantomimed the size with his hands, "instant food." He grimaced, "I never want to see instant food again." As he spoke, he snuck, under the table, bits of idiyappam to a small poodle that had joined us once lunch had been served.

As I mashed the rice noodles between my thumb and forefingers, Dias gestured at me and said in Sinhala, "The foreigner eats with her fingers." He meant that as a compliment. So my charade had been pointless. The soldiers had figured out at some point I didn't quite belong. At the edge of the parking lot, the other officer stopped to shake each of our hands. "Tell them, in Colombo, we are not bad men."

Of all my memories of that trip, I return to one most often. On the first day of our trip Major Dias had given us a tour of Kilinochchi. On the tour, at some point, a Tamil man inserted himself into our party. He was dressed in a sarong and T-shirt and wearing what they call in Sri Lanka bathroom slippers. He was gaunt and stooped slightly, and it was hard to tell his age, which could have been anywhere from forty to late sixties. As the major spoke, the Tamil man provided, in English, his own commentary—facts complimentary to the Security Forces. I could tell by the expression on the major's face that he was annoyed but he didn't stop the man or shoo him away. Eventually the man grew bored or decided he had somewhere else to be. He turned to Dias, placed his hands palms together, and bowed. "We had an old master then," he told him, "we have a new master now."

I have replayed these words again and again in my head. I can only imagine this man's suffering, but I know it was profound. And his words are both an admission of powerlessness and a plea for stewardship. As I relive the moment, trying to envision exactly what he looked like, all that he said, I also feel as if I owe that man something more than capturing him and his words eternally in an essay, of freeze-framing him in time—another moment in a travelogue. I also know now more than ever that all I am is a tourist—one that fulfilled her duty and kept her appropriate distance—and the photo album-picture moment is all I have to offer.

Abecedarian for the Abeyance of Loss

I found Kate Greenaway's *A Apple Pie* years ago while browsing in a used bookstore. When I opened the cover, I heard an echo—a woman's voice—reading to me. I spent part of my early childhood in England and that happens sometimes—I see a clip of an old British television show or I'll find a British candy bar in a bodega in Brooklyn. It is always a painful experience.

It interests me that, while abecedarians may be the most familiar literary form since almost all of us learn to read by using them, they were originally associated with spells and prayers: a mnemonic device that helped us to remember the lines and deliver the incantation even more powerfully.

This abecedarian—the words and the drawings—are an attempt to seam my memory. They are nothing more than elaborately manic doodles—the sort anyone makes while trying to pay attention to a long-winded speech. They hint at the history of illustration—a history that has long obsessed me since I trained as an artist before I started training at anything else. Aubrey Beardsley appears in this. John Singer Sargent. Alchemical drawings. Ancient Sanskrit art. And the abecedarian itself is a riff on Greenaway's *A Apple Pie*. In addition, the original rhyme for *A Apple Pie* was first published in 1671. In that version the *I* and *J* were not differentiated. The *J* was the curved initial form of the *I* and often used instead. Kate Greenaway preserved that convention in 1886 for her version of *A Apple Pie*, and I do the same now for my version.

CRAVE IT

DEAL IT

EAT IT

K KNEEL FOR IT

L LIKE IT

M MAKE YOURSELF

N NUMB TO IT

S STORE IT

T TAKE IT

UVWXYZ

HAVE A LARGE SLICE
AND
SLEEP ON IT

Amblyopia

A MEDICAL HISTORY

Force Is Equal to the Change in Momentum(mv) per Change in Time—Part I

That morning, I threw my schoolbooks in the backseat of my car—a common practice for me at the time, probably a common practice for most sixteen-year-olds. The intersection from my neighborhood to the main road was typically busy—morning rush hour—and I, relatively new to driving, probably a bit reckless, decided to take a chance and make the left turn even though the oncoming white van was traveling fast. I hit the gas, and the car lurched forward.

(Do I remember the car stalling?)

The force of the impact turned my textbooks into projectiles. One hit me in the back of the head hard enough to knock me unconscious. My sister, who was in the passenger seat, wasn't hurt, but when she looked over at me and saw me unconscious she thought I was dead.

(My mother told me later that the phone call from a neighbor to let her know there'd been an accident and the quiet on the other end when she asked if my sister and I were alright were the worst moments of her life.)

In the PICU, the neurologist informed my parents that I had possibly suffered a severe brain injury. My left pupil was permanently dilated, indicating potential brain damage. They gave my parents a choice: operate or wait to see if I woke up. But, the surgery itself was dangerous, life-threatening, and my parents decided to wait. They took turns sitting by my bedside, speaking to me in English and Sinhala. I have one memory from this time: I am semi-conscious trapped between sleep and wakefulness. My father is speaking to me: *If you don't wake up you might die.* I try to open my eyes but it's as if a heavy, gray towel has been placed over my face. That's the color, a kind of thick, liquid gray. I want to open my eyes, because my father is begging, but I can't.

I remained in a coma for three days. When I regained consciousness, my left eyelid was shut and I couldn't open it.

I Try to Use My Lazy Eye for Personal Advancement

The editor wanted fiction and essays about disability. We were thrown together by a writers' conference, and I had ten minutes to impress her. She sat next to me on a porch swing. I tried hard not to move because, every time either one of us did, the swing pitched and threw us both off balance. I mentioned that I could write something on my lazy eye. She smiled kindly and shook her head. "A lazy eye is not a disability."

I tried to explain the double vision, the weakening eyesight. The editor sported a suit jacket, her hair cut in a neat bob. She leaned toward me to make it clear she was not unsympathetic. If not for the swing, she would have reached over and patted me on the knee. "I'm looking for work by people who really have to struggle. I mean who have really persevered against some terrible odds." She spoke softly and gently, the tone of a counselor. "And your lazy eye? I wouldn't really have noticed it if you hadn't mentioned it."

I switched to describing a short story I was working on about a young boy suffering from schizophrenia.

Force Is Equal to the Change in Momentum(mv) per Change in Time—Part II

My senior year of high school. I wore an eye patch for months to cover my partially closed eye. My eyelid drooped severely and my eye itself didn't track properly up and down. This caused disorienting moments of double vision particularly when I was climbing stairs. I tripped a lot.

It was my neurologist who made me finally take the patch off because he was afraid it would cause further weakness in my left eye. *Your eye is an organ and part of a larger system. If you don't use it, the rest of the system will shut that wounded organ down.* After my parents forced me to throw away the eye patch, I grew my hair long and wore it cascading over my face, a thick black, mourning veil.

I didn't want to go to my senior prom, but my mother made me. "You'll regret it for the rest of your life if you don't." My high school prom photograph is of me in a shimmering pink shift I had my mother sew for me. My black hair covers half my face. My date is polished and handsome in a white tuxedo, corsage pinned to lapel.

My father came up with the idea, I think, of having a professional photographer take my portrait so that I'd feel better about myself. The photographer, I admit, was very good. In every photograph he made sure to position me at a slight angle so that my lazy eye wasn't noticeable. Two large portraits of me still hang in our living room and the dining room. In each, I look whole and perfect.

Our Second Date

"I think you're beautiful *because* of your lazy eye," she said to me. We sat in a bistro-style restaurant waiting for our meals, a bottle of wine between us. I didn't feel drunk exactly, more euphoric, giddy with the newness of it all. I barely knew this woman, and was still trying to learn and discern her tics and emotional tells. Typically, I limit my alcohol consumption in social situations. My eyelid droops noticeably when I'm drunk. But, I liked this person a lot, and I wanted her to be comfortable with me.

*

Women offer me this consolation: You are beautiful *because* of your lazy eye.

John Milton Receives No Answers, Part I

Ancient Arabic medicine provided two diagnoses for blindness: *gutta serena* and *gutta obscura. Gutta obscura* would now be more commonly known as a cataract. The medical equivalent today of *gutta serena* is amaurosis, vision loss that results without any lesion or trauma to the eye itself (and, therefore, the pupil remains clear).

In *Paradise Lost,* Milton describes his blindness this way:

. . . but thou
Revisit'st not these eyes that roll in vain
To find the piercing ray, and find no dawn

All the extant accounts we have about Milton's blindness indicate that he went blind relatively young—around forty-five—and that he never truly knew why, was given no explanation by two separate diagnoses: the first *gutta serena* and the other *suffusio nigra,* another term at the time for amaurosis. Both indicate that there was no apparent change in the structure of the eye itself—a cataract or glaucoma—to explain Milton's vision loss. This has been also confirmed in written accounts from a few of Milton's friends.

*

A friend, and physician, who'd known Milton in his youth described Milton's eyes, from childhood, as "none the quickest." Milton claimed to have noticed his "weak eis" as a youth. He also claimed that eye strain brought upon by studying by candlelight late into the night precipitated his blindness.

Force Is Equal to the Change in Momentum(mv) per Change in Time—Part III

My pupil is permanently dilated. This is painful in bright sunlight or a very bright room. If I don't wear sunglasses while outside, I develop acute headaches that feel as if some invisible hand has taken a chisel to my eye sockets.

My eye hurts most when I'm driving at night on a busy, multilane highway. I'm not alone in my distress, it seems. The National Highway Traffic Safety Administration receives thousands of complaints a year about the brightness of headlights. In fact, the effect of glare is of importance to the lighting industry as a whole, and the National Lighting Product Information Program has come up with a term for the pain that results from suddenly staring into a bright light: discomfort glare.

It makes me feel better to know, at least when it comes to this, I'm not alone.

As If in a Horror Movie or a Gogol Novel, My Good Eye Takes on a Life of Its Own

The phoropter gave a shudder, a click. One lens replaced the other, and the letters on the Snellen chart transformed into featureless smudges. "Worse," I announced. The optometrist sat perched on a stool, belly spilling over the waistline of his pants. His receding hairline made his ruddy, boyish face appear rounder and fuller. I couldn't tell exactly how old he was. Maybe thirty. Maybe fifty. I was late to the appointment (I went to the wrong office) and I didn't have my insurance card. About ten minutes into the visit, he informed me that when I first walked through the door he wasn't sure about me: late, missing insurance card, a lazy eye. His accent placed him as someone born and raised in the area, and his mannerisms—the way that he gently chided me—felt culturally specific to the region.

He nattered throughout the visit, providing me a rolling commentary on life in the small town we lived in. I didn't really mind because, truthfully, he was careful and interested in me, and my case. My left pupil, it turned out, was permanently deformed. Some of the muscles that dilate and constrict the pupil had healed and tried to work but other muscles remained paralyzed. As a result, my left pupil was no longer round but shaped like an Aleve caplet. The optometrist chortled when he related this to me, taken with my oddness. "It's a good thing you have very dark brown eyes, he chuckled. "Otherwise, it might be disconcerting to people." I decided then not to like him.

After about an hour of tests, he informed me that I have superb eyesight in my right eye. Better than 20/20. "Your right eye," he explained, "is compensating for the extreme weakness of the left eye."

My brain, it seems, prefers the information coming from the dominant eye and pushes down the information coming from the weak eye. Fewer signals travel the neural pathways between my lazy eye and my brain, and eventually the myelin sheath around those neurons has thinned while the sheath around the dominant eye has become thicker and a better conductor. The medical article I'm reading describes it as the dominant eye "bullying" the lazy eye—a metaphor that makes me feel sorry for my lazy eye.

As I left his office, the optometrist warned me to double check my left side when driving. "You might not see an oncoming car at an intersection or passing you." I want to get out of his office and so don't tell him that the two near-accidents I've had while driving occurred when I failed to notice a car passing along my right, my good, side.

Please Describe in Detail
Any OTHER Medical Complaints

Lennard J. Davis's history of obsession gives a detailed etymology of the word. The Latin root, *obsessionem,* means to lay siege, to block, to obstruct. Davis notes that in the 1600s obsession was used to describe a type of physical inhabitation synonymous with demonic possession. The difference though between possession and obsession was awareness. The possessed person did not know that the demon had taken control. The obsessed person, on the other hand, was aware of the demon's assault on the body and soul and therefore was expected to resist, to put up a fight. The current connotation—that of neuroses or mental illness—is a relatively new construction, traceable to the early 20th century.

I think when my date observed, his lips pursed, "You're obsessed with your lazy eye," he meant to employ the 17th-century meaning of the word. He believed me to be possessed by my insecurity and fully expected me to resist that demon so that he could have a good time. He also, I suspect now, felt besieged by what he perceived as my constant need for affirmation.

What he didn't take into consideration is that for me talking about my lazy eye is both painful and a means for me to take control of my body and the situation. I depend on the willingness of most people not to mention it. It's a form of social contract. But for me to mention it to someone provides me the deepest form of intimacy I can muster. An allowance that I know people can see it, and that it is a form of disfigurement.

"It doesn't matter to me," he assured me.

Men typically offer me this: My eye, it doesn't matter.

My (Now Ex-) Partner
When I Interrogate Him on Our Fourth Date:

"I don't know. I thought you were cute."

Ulysses S. Grant Writes a Love Letter to His Wife After She Learns the Surgeons Won't Operate to Relieve Her Strabismus

Dear Julia,

I don't want to have your eyes fooled with. They are all right as they are. They look just as they did the very first time I ever saw them—the same eyes I looked into

when I fell in love with you—the same eyes that looked
up into mine and told me that my love was returned . . .

I developed a personal fondness for Ulysses S. Grant after reading that letter so I'm glad that in the last decade his reputation
has been somewhat rehabilitated.

John Milton Receives No Answers, Part II

The best, extended description of Milton's blindness comes
from a written account he provided to a friend. This friend had
planned to give Milton's description of his illness to a famed
Parisian oculist in the hopes, perhaps, that the doctor would
agree to treat him.

In the letter, Milton gives a detailed medical history of his
experience of going blind. "It is ten years," he writes, ". . . since
I felt my sight getting weak and dull." Later he describes when
he first realized his vision loss: "If I looked at a lit candle, a kind
of iris seemed to snatch it from me. Not long after, a darkness
coming over the left part of my left eye . . . removed from my
vision all objects situated on that side." He goes on to describe
in detail a creeping loss: first he can perceive a little bit of light,
then this becomes duller, and finally darkness. But this, he clar-
ifies, "the darkness which is perpetually before me, by night as
well as by day, seems always nearer to whitish than to a black-
ish, and such that, when the eye rolls itself there is admitted, as
through a small chink a certain trifle of light."

*

Theories as to the cause of Milton's blindness have ranged from congenital syphilis, an intracranial tumor, and glaucoma. But the general consensus among doctors that care about this sort of extreme postmortem conjecture is that Milton suffered from myopia and, possibly, detached retinas, hence the bursts of light Milton reports and the loss of peripheral vision.

No, I'm not going to try to claim here that Milton really had a lazy eye. I didn't start reading Milton because of his blindness— not directly anyway. I was trying to find something else.

Coming Back from Dinner with My (Now Ex-) Partner's Brother

During our dinner we were interrupted by my partner's brother's next-door neighbor. She had a quick question that he answered in the hallway. When the brother re-entered the apartment and closed the door behind him, he made a comment about how "hot" the neighbor was. All the way back home that night, I fretted aloud about my lazy eye, about how ugly it made me. I don't think my partner made the connection. Or maybe he was just used to hearing me complain.

A Definition of an Important Medical Term

It turns out, I don't actually have amblyopia. What has happened to my eye is a severe, traumatic, permanent injury and there's no surgery or medicine that will help. I experience a nearly constant, thumping pressure in the area of my left eye socket because of the injury.

*

A neuro-ophthalmologist explained it to me this way: "We're in the business of preserving and correcting vision. Ptosis, an eye that doesn't track correctly, if it isn't affecting visual acuity, you can maybe make the presentation less severe with plastic surgery." She paused to make her point, "But we're not going to try a radical treatment for your eye, like surgery, that could adversely impact your vision, for aesthetic reasons alone."

A year ago, another ophthalmologist informed me that the visual acuity in my left eye is deteriorating.

My Mother Suggests I Use My Amblyopia for Financial Gain

In the mid-'90s, my mother called me and suggested I join a class action lawsuit filed against Ford. The lawsuit claimed that Ford knew of defective parts, used in their Escorts, that caused the cars to stall suddenly and unpredictably during acceleration.

My mother was a good businesswoman. She never missed an opportunity to make money. I'm surprised though that my mother wanted me to join the lawsuit. She knew I was insecure about the lazy eye and that I spent many years trying to find a surgeon willing to try to fix it. Each one refused to operate on an otherwise healthy eye.

*

I pointed out to her days later, after having done a little research, "You have to be able to say you suffered some monetary loss. That you can't work, for example."

"Thatha and I think you should claim you're never going to get married because of it." I told her I had to go and hung up.

Corrected Diagnosis

One doctor explained to me that the exact name of my eye disorder is Horner's syndrome. Horner's syndrome results from trauma to the sympathetic nerve system that runs along the spine at the back of the neck. Among the symptoms of Horner's syndrome, constriction of the pupil and partial ptosis.

The doctor acted vaguely irritated by my ignorance. Apparently, she only treated patients who knew exactly what was wrong with them.

Minutes later she mused as she wrote in my chart, "Sometime Horner's syndrome gets better suddenly." It wasn't clear if this was an attempt to provide me hope or if she was thinking aloud.

A decade later another doctor tells me that this doctor wasn't entirely correct. The injury is more complicated than that. This news doesn't exactly surprise me. Personally, I long ago settled for lazy eye to describe it. I like the censorious feel, like I'm calling my eye a terrible name, separating it from the rest of me like Gogol's "nose."

Maybe My Mother Was Right About One Thing

In 2001, Ford settled with the claimants in the class action suit for 2.7 billion dollars.

Our Third Date

"I'm not sure how I feel about femmes," she said. I shook my head. "Women who need to meet certain cultural beauty standards." She spoke generally. She never mentioned my lazy eye, and I'm not sure she liked me enough to really notice.

My Google Search for Celebrities Who Suffer from Amblyopia Generates a List

Paris Hilton	Heidi Klum	Zac Efron
Ryan Gosling	Kristen Bell	Taylor Lautner
Alicia Keys	Hugh Grant	Jeff Bezos
Steve Buscemi	Thom Yorke	Topher Grace

The person compiling this list had not hacked these celebrities' medical histories. They guessed, it seems, after staring a long time at celebrity photographs.

It occurs to me now that all these celebrities are, or have been, married. Most have been married multiple times. So, about this, my mother was wrong.

Two Weeks into Our Relationship

He put his arm around me and declared, "You're my little space oddity."

Forms of Exercise I Do with a Lazy Eye

Running	Step Aerobics	Archery	Yoga
Walking	Hiking	Spinning	Kayaking
Swimming	Weight Training	Zumba	Ping-pong

What I Won't Do Because of My Lazy Eye

Ride a bike

Processes That I Have to Modify Because of My Lazy Eye

The disjunction between my right and left eye feels most pronounced when I'm trying to draw. The constant awareness that my left eye is tracking far more slowly than my right, feels a bit like seasickness. To ease the discomfort, I sometimes cover my left eye with a patch.

When I first started drawing this way, patch over one eye, I encountered another problem. Because of the lack of depth perception, the pen tip or the paintbrush didn't land where I wanted. I missed the spot by millimeters. It disconcerted me to think my hand was moving toward one spot and see it actually hit another. When I was in grade school, our insult of choice was "spastic." When these moments of misapplication happened to me, I always imagined a child's voice, petty and immature, taunting me, *Spaz!*

But, when drawing from life, many artists momentarily cover one eye in order to flatten an image and correctly judge proportion. In *Six Drawing Lessons,* the artist William Kentridge suggests drawing with one eye closed as an exercise. He never explains why, but he also believes in a concept he calls mistranslation—that our mistakes and slight errors bring out what's real and intuitive in our work.

The Couple Next to Me on the Flight to Sri Lanka

We'd been laughing and chatting and drinking together for most of the nine-hour flight when the woman leaned into me and said, "My husband and I think you're lovely. We're staying at Galle Face. Maybe you'll give us a call? If you want to party?"

Some Random Man

"You look like a girl that's been punched in the face a couple of times." This, I think, is his way of letting me know he is interested in me.

My Mother and Father Take Me on a Pilgrimage Because of My Lazy Eye

When I was eighteen, my grandmother wrote and asked my parents to take me on a pilgrimage to the temple in Kataragama,

Sri Lanka. My grandmother was a well-educated woman but superstitious, and she suggested to my mother that my lazy eye was a result of some evil influence—someone's jealousy. The pilgrimage would earn me merit.

The idea annoyed me at first—it would be a reminder to everyone that I wasn't quite whole—and I put off the pilgrimage until my early twenties. By then, I had grown more interested in my Sri Lankan identity, and I was curious about what a pilgrimage would entail. I'd also experienced a particular trauma that had had something to do with my lazy eye, or so I thought, and it seemed to me possible that my grandmother wasn't wrong—there existed some terrible influence at work in my life.

I had been to Buddhist temples before, but I had never been to a site like Kataragama. It isn't uncommon in Asia for a holy shrine to be used by multiple religions, and Kataragama is holy for the Sinhalese and Tamils. Buddhist temples can be busy places but nothing like the throngs I witnessed at Kataragama. In fact, I've never participated in anything like it. I kept a journal of the trip, but can no longer find it, and, perhaps because of jet lag, or just time, my memories are vague: A wall of people, all thrilled and celebrating, joyous. A lot of fire. Candles, oil lamps, aarti lamps. Frangipani petals, wilting beneath the statues of the Lord Buddha and Lord Krishna. And, of course, strings of decorative lights hanging, a thatched canopy. By nightfall, a thin fragrant mist sheathed the temple grounds. The still lingering emotion is one of awe.

In fact, in retrospect, the whole pilgrimage was, I have no other word for it, fun. We were accompanied by another family, and the entire voyage—all of us crammed into a small van—was raucous and buoyant. They didn't mention my eye—though I imagine they knew that was why we were traveling together—and even though we all experienced the discomforts associated with traveling in a developing country there was a great deal of camaraderie.

I recognize how important this trip must have been for my parents. It gave them the opportunity to partake in a cultural ritual with me, a ritual they knew from their childhoods, that wasn't about the failures of medicine, or their own inadequacies as parents trying to fix a broken child. The pilgrimage was ancient, magic, imbued with the power of gods. I perceived none of this at the time. Throughout the trip, I experienced fits of rage whenever I was alone. All I understood, until I was in the temple itself, was that I was being ritually humiliated for becoming ugly.

My one real memory of the trip—the one that remains vivid—is not of Kataragama but of another temple on the road to the larger, much more famous shrine. I stood just outside of the temple in front of a large cave whose walls, thick and black, rippled like a curtain. It appeared to me as if the face of the hill had been caught for eternity in one long, terrified, silent scream. I asked my father what was happening. He pushed me forward and I stumbled because I didn't want to go nearer the gaping, rippling, maw. Thousands of tiny specks, like ash, expressed into the air, a fetid breath, and, then, were swallowed. Bats, my uncle laughed from the van. An optical illusion, my father offered. The walls of the cave were covered by thousands of bats: sleeping, hunting, cavorting. I laughed when I realized what I was looking at, but the unsettled moment when I couldn't discern what I was witnessing is what stays with me decades later.

I Harass My Mother About Finding Someone Who Will Fix My Lazy Eye

My parents and I had consulted multiple ophthalmologists, all who refused to operate. The latest one had been kind but insistent. A legitimate surgeon would not put my eyesight in jeopardy.

I was distraught during the car ride home, and livid, I berated my mother for not being willing to find someone who would help me. My mother stared over the steering wheel, sorrowful and quiet. Finally, she explained to me that according to Buddhism nothing was permanent and there were so many people who had lost far more.

This sent me into a cascade of vituperation. I hated Buddhism. I hated the backward town and state where I lived where there was no one good enough to help me. And most of all I hated her. She had never loved me enough because a mother who loved you fixed you.

A red light and the car slowed to a stop. I must have needed to catch a breath, carried away by all my rage. My mother took the moment to respond. "You have to understand," she said. The light from a passing car slid across her face. "For three days I thought you were going to die. For me, it's enough that you're alive."

*

At the time, that was *not* nearly enough for me. I hated her more for trying to transpose her lesser pain over mine, lesser because she had gotten what she wanted. I hadn't.

On the Eve of the Demise of a 13-Year Relationship

Dinner in a Korean restaurant with my partner. We'd been together, off and on, for a long time and we had recently recommitted to each other. Seven months earlier I'd moved in with him.

My bowl of bibimbap was half eaten. I'm not even sure what we were fighting about, but we fought all the time by then. About five years before he'd temporarily lost vision in one eye and had undergone a series of very painful surgeries. His mother had also passed away around the same time as his eye surgery. She'd suffered a form of Parkinson's that progressed quickly, and, before her death, he'd helped his father to care for her while she rapidly lost control of her body. He had even, at times, changed her diapers. I knew, from day-to-day life with him, these were constant traumas that had woven themselves deeply into his sense of self and security.

At the dinner, I railed about my lazy eye. I can't remember what he'd said specifically, but my punishment was to assail him with my own woundedness. How ugly it made me feel. How ugly I must have appeared to him. This wasn't the first time I'd done this. I'd gone on these sorts of rants throughout our relationship, and once I started there was nothing he could say to make me feel better.

*

In the middle of my diatribe, he closed his eyes. I noticed that smudges underneath his eyes, the sallow skin. He looked unhealthy, but I knew the truth. He was depressed. He spoke slowly. "You know one day, you're going to be really sick, and you're going to look back at this time in your life, at this moment, and regret not realizing that your lazy eye was nothing. It isn't the cause of anything wrong in your life."

Why I Am Obsessing on John Milton's Blindness

In a class on John Milton, the professor told us that Milton taught his daughters Latin and Greek so that they could read to him and so that he could dictate to them large portions of *Paradise Lost* and *Paradise Regained*. He was, the professor said, quite cruel to his children. The professor believed this was an indication of Milton's misogyny, which I don't doubt, but I also recognized something else in the story, the spitefulness of a man enraged by loss. The blind keeping those around him blind.

We like to imagine the blind Milton as a man at peace with his loss, made dignified by his pain, capable of writing "They also serve who only stand and wait." We read through his careful rendering of his medical history and marvel at his pragmatic descriptions of what must have been a terrible trauma. But there is also an equally well-documented Milton as a man gripped by a deep and untenable fury. The swing between these two personas is so severe that it forms the basis of the conjecture that he suffered from congenital syphilis. What I never found was an explanation that attributed his cruelty to his attempts to live with his profound loss.

*

I'm drawn to the rage—even though I'm aware that any attempt to ascribe it to an inability to accept his blindness is, at best, an educated guess. I'm drawn to it because I see much of myself in it. All the furiousness, the desire to crush others. The truth is I have always despised the attempts to console me. In those moments, I feel a bitterness so acute it is, for a second, like a screen passing over my vision. I taste bitterness, like blood, at the back of my throat. No one has ever made me feel better. A few have made me feel worse. The only two people who have ever truly reached me in my rage—my mother and my ex—had to be pummeled into begging me to understand their own pain. But those were not attempts to placate. They are both testimonials to a great love under duress.

I won't recount Milton's treatment of his daughters. Several biographies, works of fiction, and even a play explore their relationship. But this revisioning of Milton is a late 20th-century reckoning. Prior to the 20th century, Milton's daughters were held up as exemplars. There exist several paintings, all by male artists, that depict dutiful teenage women at the feet of handsome, stoic middle-aged men: images of filial duty painted to instruct.

I found one print that has stayed with me. It's different from the rest. Yes, one daughter is focused, transcribing her father's words. In every other way, though, the etching deviates from most portraits of Milton. The great poet sits in a shadow and looks haggard. He stares off at the wrong point, and his body is cocooned in a heavy, black cape. He appears vampiric. In the center of the etching, a second daughter is looking up and she faces the viewer. One arm is thrust forward to protect herself. Her lips are slightly pursed, eyes askance. Sunlight from a nearby window cascades over her, turning her blonde hair into a halo. But it's the expression on her face that I try to understand. She doesn't appear unhappy but she isn't doting either. She looks, in fact, defiant—as if considering recording the wrong words. It's as if the artist, and I've never been able to find a name, knows: to serve a blind man is not a privilege but an ordeal of its own.

It is a problematic portrait of disability—the praise of wholeness and youth over the selfishness of age and eventual degeneration—but I return to it again and again, as a reminder, as the prescription.

PART II

. . . AND RECOVERY

Soft Target

i.

If I talk about Chicago, I tend to lie. I lied most recently two years ago at a party. I didn't know many of the attendees. I had drifted to a far corner of the living room where I hoped to hide until a reasonable time had passed, and I could leave without seeming impolite. A colleague of mine at the university where I teach and his partner found me there and, buzzed from the adrenaline rush that comes from socializing, giddy, and cosseted in a warm corner, we started confessing about past sexual dalliances.

They were explaining to me the dangers of cruising. Maybe, I just wanted to prove that I could keep up, or that I was open or open-minded, or I just wanted to be part of the group, but I blurted, "I was a bit of a slut in my twenties and thirties." I raised my nearly empty plastic cup of soda water as if about to give a toast. "I did stupid things." And then I added, "Sometimes I'm surprised I'm still alive."

They both smiled gamely. I was laughing and, anyway, I was carried away. "There was a time in London when I was invited to a party by a man I barely knew." And with that, I had changed the country: England. I changed the city: London. I didn't change one element: that a man I knew as an acquaintance took me to a party and when we arrived I realized that it wasn't so much a party as a small gathering of only men in a remote area of the city that wasn't easily accessed by public transportation. I smiled all the way through my embroidered and embellished story. I made it funny. I made myself partly clueless but also resourceful and believably tough. I added the presence of two women. It embarrasses me now how deeply and gleefully I lied. At this temporal distance, I recognize that it makes me appear a little nutty.

I changed the ending of my story too: I said that the acquaintance, when he realized I was uncomfortable, cared about me enough to call me a taxi and send me home.

ii.

For part of the seven months I spent in Chicago, when I was twenty, I sheered my hair close to the scalp. This opened my face up and made the drooping eyelid even more noticeable. I was small breasted and big-hipped. My short hair made my already round face seem fuller, something like the slightly mis-shapen heads of those cheap golden Buddha's populating road-side shrines in my home country. I wore men's Polo shirts and jeans and sneakers, and a Yankee baseball cap turned backwards. I sported only one earring—a fairy. When I described what I was like to a friend recently, he started singing, "Rebel, rebel your face is a mess." Like that? Yes. Except in the song, she (or is it he) is the hero. But I was plain and androgynous—not in a cool, David Bowie way—more in an unhappy, slightly troubled way.

People regularly referred to me as sir. Once, as I was strolling along the Gold Coast after visiting a friend, a police cruiser slowed down next to me until the officers were able to capture a glimpse of my face. They turned their heads slowly, the hard set of the jaw, and stared straight ahead when they realized I was not a threat.

I was awkward, unremarkable and, worse, immature. No one—not men, not women—hit on me, ever. This didn't have anything to do with my looks and probably more to do with my essential awkwardness. I didn't get the things other young, female friends of mine living in a big city received: free dinners, elaborate and expensive gifts, love letters. But there existed a part of me that felt protected by this lack of attention. My instructors at the School of the Art Institute of Chicago, mostly men, assumed I was a lesbian and while, honestly, I minded that at first, it made me feel exposed, I didn't correct them.

All through high school, I crushed on boys and girls. I became obsessed with the possibility that I was really meant to be a boy but the only terms I had at my disposal to express this were tomboy or butch lesbian, and I didn't feel comfortable with either of those identities. I wasn't athletic enough to be a tomboy and to add butch lesbian to my outsider immigrant status would have meant complete ostracization from straight society, or so I imagined. I couldn't, at that point, handle casting away every culture I had ever known. I confessed to teachers that I felt different, but I never had the imagination, or the yearning, to actually be physically a boy. Still, I didn't think like any of the girls I knew—for one thing I wasn't desperate to have sex with a boy—or share their values: a belief in my prettiness, a willingness to flirt, a desire to make a boy happy. My first real love was a woman. But I hadn't kissed anyone until college, when I was seventeen.

By my late teens, I had translated my oddness into a deep commitment to feminism. I was obsessed with Judy Chicago and her *Dinner Party,* and aimed to be a woman artist that took on, and deconstructed, the masculine gaze. As an art student at UNC-Chapel Hill, a group of artists and I papier-mâchéd our torsos and created a giant indoor chandelier of breasts that hung above the heads of people entering the art building. An art professor of mine pointed to the cast of my torso, "That's you. I can tell because of the way the back curves." I experience, simultaneously, annoyance at his failure to recognize our defiance and a feeling that I had deserved the comment somehow.

I drew Conté crayon nudes, drawn from life onto long strips torn from brown paper rolls, that made women's bodies appear epic, imposing landscapes. I left my home in North Carolina not just to study art, but because I imagined for myself a bohemian, outré lifestyle even if I didn't quite have the courage, or the facility, to make that lifestyle come about.

And, if I had had the right language, I think I would have referred to myself as gender nonbinary and asexual. I wish for my former self I could have done that. But neither of those terms existed for me then, and without the words to describe, to define, to place the parameters of what you are, you can't truly perform, or even claim, an identity.

iii.

The Art Institute is in in the heart of the Chicago loop and didn't, at that time, offer student housing, so I found a room at the Eleanor Residence: a woman's-only group home not far from Lincoln Park. My room was just large enough to fit a dresser, a table, a twin bed, and a small sink. I shared a bathroom with the other women on my hall. We didn't have phones in our rooms—this was well before cell phones—and had to use a payphone, tucked in a large wooden phone booth, in the hallway. The residence had been founded in the early 1920s, and some of the rules hadn't changed in seventy years. Men were only allowed in the building at certain times and, even then, had to remain in a parlor area. They couldn't visit us in our rooms.

Some of the women in the hall were students. A few were professionals trying to establish themselves or completing temporary assignments that required a few-months stay in the city. I remember one resident who had lived there a few years. She was beautiful, in her early thirties, tall and blonde. She worked and seemed to make a high enough salary that she could find a place on her own, and Eleanor Residence wasn't cheap. She didn't try to find her own place during the time I lived there. At dinner in the cafeteria, in the television room, the residents talked about men: meeting men, attracting men, dating men, marrying men. We talked about our waists, or weights, and most of all we compared each other's beauty as a man might perceive it. I had never really before that spent so much time talking about my body and men but, new to the city and without many friends, I didn't want to be left out. Our fixation seems excessive in retrospect, and I wonder if we weren't all working double-time to dispel what we imagined were the whispers about the residence hall—that it was an enclave for dykes, or worse: that we were broken somehow.

We were only a few blocks from Lake Michigan. I had arrived there in late August, and so for most of my stay the lake was shrouded in winter fog and mist. On some mornings, the mist and fog hung so thick that it looked as if the city was perched on nothing more substantial than a large cloud. Other days the water stretched out, an expanse of smooth, hard slate. That's my memory of Chicago—a constant grayness, a hard, unending slab of a city. The first time I waited for a bus in the winter, the cold gnashed through my winter coat and gloves. The tips of my fingers and my feet froze so painfully that I thought as I boarded that I might have frostbite. And there was that ever-present wind that felt like a giant hand pressing against my back, trying to push me down. I was miserable for most of my stay. I still don't tell people I lived in Chicago, and, recently, when the city came up in a conversation I pretended as if I'd never even visited. At this point, almost thirty years on, I have no reason to tell anyone I've been there, and it's easier than having to explain what feels now a failure.

The first few weeks at the residence, a female jogger was attacked in Lincoln Park. Two police officers lectured a group of us, new to the city, about how to stay safe. They warned us not to make ourselves soft targets. Don't use purses or bags with cross-body straps. Don't pull your wallet out in public and reveal how much money you have. Think about the way you stand. Think about the way you dress. A tight skirt makes it harder to fight back or run. One of the officers—a short, stocky woman with the practiced no-nonsense disdain of the seasoned law enforcement officer—told us that a serial rapist had once explained, after getting caught, how he picked his victims: "He chose women who couldn't meet his gaze when he passed them." The officer's tone admonished not the rapist but the silly, weak woman who had glanced down at the sidewalk. Up to that point, I knew I tended to avert my gaze when I passed people. It was not as if they really saw me anyway. But after that I practiced keeping my head up when I walked by someone, especially a man.

iv.

I'm bisexual, but in truth I'm not always sure what it means to say that beyond I've slept with men and women and will very likely sleep with both again. I've never really located my sex life around an identity, and I've typically thought of myself simply as very fluid, and as I described myself in another essay, willing. For the longest time, I didn't think that was enough to form a political self. I live and work now in a rural area, and the community I serve has a large number of LGBTQ youth in need of mentoring. I started expressly referring to myself as queer because I wanted my students to know that I share not only a set of experiences with them but an allegiance.

I mentioned to a friend recently that I was going on a date with a woman. "You know I'm bisexual, yes?"

She shrugged. "I assume most people are." I would have said the same thing a few years ago.

This ambivalence bothers me now. In my late twenties, and in my thirties, when I admitted being bisexual to friends or lovers, I really still framed it within the expectations of a straight, male society. I was, to quote Adrienne Rich, an Anna, "who invited defeat from men without ever being conscious of it." Adrienne Rich in her essay "Compulsory Heterosexuality and Lesbian Experience" argues heterosexuality is not merely a biological choice but a political institution, one that often violently suppresses a woman's image of her own sexuality and libido to allow men continual and unfettered access to women's bodies. But she also cautions against positing that the opposite of compulsory heterosexuality is bisexuality or even homosexuality. The opposite of compulsory heterosexuality, according to Rich, is the existence of political and cultural institutions that celebrate and make visible the emotional and erotic relationships between women and that focus solely on women. I struggle with the possibility that Rich is right. If I'd wanted to truly fight for change, I'd have lived by and fought for her vision. And, I can't tell anymore if I've been brave, or dumb, or just always somehow complicit.

V.

I don't really remember what he looked like, except that he was short, slim, and small-made, and I don't remember his name. He was a fellow student at the Art Institute, and I know I had a crush on him, but he showed little interest in me beyond friendship. I went to his apartment because I was hanging out with him as a friend, one of the few I had made in Chicago outside the residence hall. I don't remember the ride to the apartment or anything prior to the apartment—a date at a coffeeshop or dinner. I do have a vague recollection of sitting on a couch and sharing a take-out pizza—or maybe it was Chinese food. I can't remember if I started drinking in his apartment, but I must have been because I don't know what else would make my memory of the rest of that evening so hazy.

Early in the evening, two of his friends—two men—stopped by. I had never seen them before, and as hard as I try the only image I can conjure is two silhouettes—one lanky and slim, the other much shorter—standing in the hallway. I don't know if they knew I was there before they arrived. They played off their arrival at his place as something casual, and my friend acted as if he hadn't expected them. They asked if I wanted to go to a party. I know that they used this word because I do have a memory of my impression of where they wanted to take me. I'm not incautious. I live with the same fears of sexual assault as most women in our culture. But this was a fellow student, and the Art Institute was actually small in comparison to my last school—we all knew each other. I imagined a party to look something like the parties I'd attended before in frat houses at UNC-Chapel Hill and residences off-campus, parties attended mostly by friends and acquaintances. Or maybe I, already lazy-eyed, South Asian, socially awkward, didn't want to add to that list uncool.

The car I got into was a sedan. I don't know what make or model, and I didn't look at the license plate. My friend and the other two guys didn't talk a lot. At some point during the drive, I realized they were making a lot of turns, and the streets had become unfamiliar to me. We stopped to buy alcohol. The store was a large cement box. It was my first time inside a liquor store with a bullet-proof barricade protecting the cashier. That's why I remembered it. The cashier placed the bottles on a carousel and barely looked at us. I didn't know where I was—in what neighborhood or area of Chicago—or where I was being taken. I also didn't want to be so uncool as to ask.

Recently, I called my ex-partner who has known me since my mid-twenties. I asked him if he remembered me saying anything to him about what happened in Chicago. After a moment's silence, he said he did. "You told me a story when we first met."

"Do you remember what I told you?" I hoped I had related to him details then that I'd forgotten now.

"You were really vague," he replied, "but it worried me at the time." He hesitated. "I let it go. You didn't bring it up again."

Kierkegaard divides a life into two basic acts: repetition and recollection. Repetition, he claims, is something akin to ritual, while recollection is essentially the search for knowledge. Repetition brings us happiness; recollection, the minute we start engaging in it, makes us unhappy. Kierkegaard doesn't consider that we often, because we cannot really help it, make a ritual out of recollection and that this ritual is painful and ugly, ceaseless, never teaching us anything and yet we persist.

vi.

I have taped to the inside of my Moleskin datebooks the same postcard, a photograph of Carson McCullers. She is wearing a pristinely white, men's Oxford shirt. Both hands are raised above her head. The right hand holds what looks to me like a cigarette though the image is cut off. The left hand grips the right wrist as if it means to wrestle the other arm down. She looks out at the photographer, her large eyes conveying both weariness and hurt. Her lips are drawn tight. It's a pose that signals both resistance and openness, and I find the photograph strangely sexy, an image of submission transformed by its very publicness to an expression of power.

In high school, I was obsessed with McCullers. I imagined her as a fifteen-year-old girl, like me, who had somehow, unlike me, written books. I also imagined she died shortly after finishing her last book, probably at the age of sixteen. Maybe it was because unlike the other female Southern writers we were reading, Flannery O'Connor and Eudora Welty, none of our teachers taught her biography. None of our teachers, not one of them, taught us that she was bisexual and often became involved in—perhaps consciously sought to create—one love triangle after another (though I also understand that they may very well have not known about this part of her). According to the writer Sarah Schulman, McCullers might have today come out as a transgender male. Schulman offers as evidence McCullers's declaration to Truman Capote that she thought she had been born a boy.

A year or so ago, when I first thought I might want to write a longer essay about McCullers, I stumbled on a story related in a piece of academic criticism. When an elderly Carson McCullers first met the writer Gordon Langley Hall, according to Hall's account, she studied him for some time and then later whispered, "You're really a little girl." I imagine the scene: a witchy, wizened McCullers—patron saint to all of us trying to reconcile our queerness—delivering in her nasally Southern twang her diagnosis. Maybe she would recognize me too.

Langley Hall went on to claim that Carson McCullers was right. Hall was assigned the wrong sex at birth and was told later by a doctor that she had the internal sexual organs of a woman. She underwent sex reassignment surgery, changed her name to Dawn Pepita Hall, married an African American man (the first interracial marriage in South Carolina), and became a larger-than-life personality, mixing an exuberant queerness with a Southern Gothic oddness that earned her a place in profiles in *GQ* and *This American Life*.

All of Langley Hall's performances came at a cost to her though. A number of journalists began to question her story of being born intersex (and the story did change over time). She divorced her husband, and he was later committed to a mental hospital. She became estranged from many of her friends and family. She died in poverty. The journalist who spent the most time chronicling her story suggests that Langley Hall crossed so many boundaries, resisted so many social restrictions, that she ended up isolating herself from any community, even any subaltern community, that might have accepted her. She did receive a long obituary in the *New York Times*: "Dawn Langley Simmons, Flamboyant Writer, Dies at 77." In this extended celebration of Langley Hall's oddity, there is never any recognition that some of it, maybe all of it, stems from possible physical, and most certainly, emotional pain.

I suspect now that Langley Hall's story about her encounter with McCullers is an invention—a way of affirming what she perceived of as her status as freak. Langley Hall is full of such stories. For me, the real point isn't if the story is true or not. The academic I mentioned earlier opens with Langley Hall's story of McCullers because she wants to endow McCullers with the ability to recognize, both in life and art, people who deviated from the norm, especially gender norms. But both McCullers and Langley Hall's lives were not exalted tales of Gothic freakiness performed with self-knowledge but lived accounts of individuals forced to exist along the fringes. McCullers wittingly or unwittingly pursued women incapable of reciprocating her sexual interest, and she most likely lied about the one sexual experience with a woman she claimed to have had. Langley Hall should never have needed a benediction, invented or otherwise, from Carson McCullers. If she were born today, she would be considered transgender, could claim a transgender identity, she could acknowledge, if she chose, being assigned male at birth, and find some safety and visibility in a community that would see her not as odd but as powerful. And all the lies and fabrications (I hope) would be acknowledged as indications of a larger, deeper social and cultural damage. But that was not the world she lived in then.

vii.

The house was nearly empty of furniture. There was a couch, an armchair, and a wooden coffee table. I have no memory of what the outside looked like or of walking inside. I do recall at some point counting five, maybe six, men. That's it. I didn't recognize any of them. My friend had accompanied us in the car, but I don't have a memory of him in the house, of him talking to the other men or me, or him sitting with us. But that doesn't mean anything. My memory of the evening is hazy and fragmented. I can invoke a handful of images.

This is what I recall, though I'm not sure of the temporal order: I drank a lot. I didn't want anyone to think I was scared because that would mean losing control of the situation. I made myself throw up so I could drink more. I lay down on the cool tile floor of the bathroom because at least in the bathroom no one would bother me. I also recognized that if I stayed in the bathroom too long I would draw attention to myself, and I didn't want to do that. I made out with one of the men, in front of the others. I have a memory of sitting on another man's lap. I remember him most clearly. He had long dark hair—Jim Morrison-like—and he was young, in his mid-twenties. He smelled of smoke. He kept his face close to mine, his mouth on my face and neck. His arm wrapped around my waist and he spoke to me soothingly. He showed me a Buffalo penny, which he placed in the palm of my hand. After that, I don't have any recollection. All that exists is a long blank space of time. As hard as I try, I have no memory of leaving the house, or the drive back to my friend's apartment.

I woke up the next morning in my friend's bed. He made a big show of having slept on the floor. My body and my head hurt, and I was unsteady on my feet.

I didn't stay long. My friend acted cold, disinterested, and he wanted me to leave. "You look like you've been beaten up," is all he said. I have one last memory—of me sitting on the edge of my twin bed later that evening, turning the Buffalo penny again and again between my fingers. I examined my body to see if I had had sex but the only sensations that I was truly aware of was my extreme nausea and the thick wedge of pain between my eye sockets. I had a couple of bruises on my legs and arms, the sort that anyone who drinks to the point of unconscious-ness endures. Those bruises might, for all I knew, have existed before the party. I convinced myself that I hadn't had sex, that someone at the party, my friend, the guy with the long hair, had looked out for me. I held onto the penny for years before eventually throwing it away.

It took me days really to accept how terrible that evening had been, but, even then, I didn't know what to do with that awareness. I couldn't imagine walking into the dean's office at my school, much less a police station, and saying that I got into a car whose make, model, or color I couldn't remember and was driven to somewhere in the city that I couldn't point out, couldn't even specify if it was east, west, north, south. I doubted I'd been raped, and I hadn't suffered any physical injury. I didn't remember names or faces. I'd have to single out the only person who I did remember, who up to that point I had hoped might befriend me. All I could actually testify to was drinking so excessively that whole sections of my own memory had been erased. For a long time—two decades, to be exact—I told myself, even as I struggled to remember what happened, that I had no memory or proof of forced sexual intercourse. More precisely, I believed I had survived the best I knew how: a night of compromises and concessions negotiated with my flawed body. The crime, very possibly, was my own.

I never spoke to that friend again. He didn't call me that day, and I didn't try to reach out to him. A few weeks later, I found a phone message from him in my mailbox at the Eleanor Residence: an invitation to another party with him and his friends that evening. The message used that exact language: a party with him and his friends. I read it to myself so many times I memorized it. I stood in front of the row of mailboxes, pink message slip in hand, trembling. I threw the message away a few days later. I never called him back.

In the absence of any retrievable sensations, thoughts, or impressions, anything I insert in the blanks, in the blacked-out hours, is invention. But what remains, and remains painful, is the fragmented awareness of needing to perform and everything that being forced to perform implies: that I was lesser, not valuable as a person. What if my friend had told his friends ahead of time I would be there at his apartment? What if their arrival wasn't an accident? Maybe he hadn't wanted our time together to appear a date. Or he knew exactly where the three of them were planning to take me. He saw in me a naïve, vulnerable girl who could easily be coerced.

A few weeks after that evening, I found a small church at the end of the block, and I started attending services regularly. The minister, everyone who worked at the church, was kind, very liberal, and would have welcomed anyone who identified as queer without question, but I was interested in presenting myself as straight and as likeable as possible. I wanted to disappear. I was baptized at that church, saved and born again. I started wearing mostly skirts. I threw out my combat boots. I splurged on an expensive, high-end tube of lipstick. I still remember the color—a bold magenta that the salesclerk promised matched my skin type. I grew my hair out. I gave up any ambition of being an artist. I left Chicago that May.

viii.

I confessed to my colleague that I had fabricated parts of the story I had told him and his partner. We were having dinner in the school cafeteria, and, because we both teach creative nonfiction, we were talking about gender and sexual violence. I think for some time I had felt bad and wanted to come clean. I hesitated and then I admitted, "I kind of lied about something that happened."

He knew immediately what I was referring to: *that story about the party.* I was surprised at how quickly he remembered and embarrassed. I asked him if he'd guessed at the party that I was lying. He shook his head, "I believed you. I was relieved, I guess. I thought that you were incredibly lucky." He also explained to me, a few days later, that he'd made the connection so quickly because, as a nonfiction teacher, he was used to hearing people elide, erase, try to make events and incidents appear better than the truth. He also, he explained, didn't judge.

Lucky. Luck. Luck with its etymological roots in destiny and fortune implies some outside force that is on your side. If that's the case, I am *lucky.* I feel like so much of my trajectory—career, cultural, sexual—has been the result not of choice or deliberation but of a series of evasions, near misses, stumbles, and, too often, a deep inability to perceive clearly. But I am, after everything, whole.

These days I receive in my social media feed stories, written mostly by women, about the perceived invisibility of becoming middle-aged. Each time I read the clickbait ledes I think of Rich, McCullers, Langley Hall, my younger self, what invisibility meant to each of us, how it served as a force that defined us *all* our lives, and I marvel. What a privilege to have ever known who you are, to be seen and appreciated, loved, for it. But, perhaps, I'm still getting it wrong. It really doesn't matter who notices me anymore. The trick, I know now, is to be the one to level the crosshairs, to keep my head up no matter what, to meet the oncoming gaze, and, without wavering, be the one who looks back.

The Answer Key

1. Homosexual 2. Lesbian 3. Dyke 4. Intersex 5. Merci Mack 6. Drag queen 7. Bull dagger 8. What's the tea? 9. Havelock Ellis 10. Oscar Wilde 11. Faggot 12. *The Advocate* 13. Sappho 14. Pansexual 15. Drag king 16. Intersectional 17. Polyamory 18. Bisexual 19. Scissoring 20. Blowjob 21. Muff diver 22. Dildo 23. Rainbow flag 24. Brandon Teena 25. Rimming 26. *Angels in America* 27. Clitoris 28. Boston Marriage 29. Beard 30. Butt plug 31. Matthew Shephard 32. Sigmund Freud 33. ACT UP 34. Gay bar 35. Fruitcake 36. Butch dyke 37. Bottom 38. Yass! 39. Tucking 40. Binding 41. Judith Butler 42. Lesbian toaster 43. Handkerchief code 44. Gender nonconforming 45. In the closet 46. Queen 47. Fag 48. The West Village 49. Eat pussy 50. Andrew Halloran 51. Tranny 52. AIDS 53. Ronald Reagan 54. Internalized homophobia 55. Gay bar 56. *The Yellow Book* 57. Penis ring 58. Cum 59. Aromantic 60. YMCA 61. Gay Men's

Health Crisis 62. Gender nonbinary 63. Asexual 64. Eat
out 65. Dustin Parker 66. Yampi Méndez Arocho 67.
Unicorn 68. Audre Lorde 69. Gender queer 70. *Law-
rence v. Texas* 71. Lavender Scare 72. Edith Ellis 73. Fairy
74. Down low 75. Gertrude Stein 76. Montgomery Clift
77. Gay-related immune deficiency 78. Walt Whitman
79. They/Their/Theirs 80. *Hedgewig and the Angry Inch*
81. Vibrator 82. James Baldwin 83. AC/DC 84. Drag ball
85. Stonewall uprising 86. Leslie Feinberg 87. Sexology
88. Lesbian separatist movement 89. Ace 90. *The Straight
Mind* 91. Cruising 92. *Heathers* 93. Butch 94. Pansy 95.
Camp 96. *Gender Trouble* 97. Melodrama 98. Cock-
sucker 99. Fag hag 100. Switch hitter 101. Femme 102.
Stuck Rubber Baby 103. Larry Kramer 104. Coming out
105. Heterosexual 106. Bear 107. Aubrey Beardsley 108.
Misgendering 109. Rock Hudson 110. Patricia High-
smith 111. Nancy 112. Sexual inversion 113. Gay icon 114.
Marjorie Garber 115. Executive order 10450 116. Harvey
Milk 117. *Out* magazine 118. Vice versa 119. Versace 120.
Family values 121. Anal beads 122. Alexander Chee 123.
Pink Flamingo 124. Blazer 125. *Zami: A New Spelling of
My Name, A Biomythography* 126. Cross dresser 127.
BDSM 128. Erotica 129. Bisexual plot 130. *The Crying
Game* 131. Ardhanarishvara 132. Bromance 133. Green
carnations 134. *My Beautiful Laundrette* 135. Bitch 136.
Lipstick lesbian 137. Outing 138. Ponce 139. *Cunt: A Dec-
laration of Independence* 140. *My Tender Matador* 141.
David Wojnarowicz 142. Lambda Legal 143. *Romer v
Evans* 144. Robert Mapplethorpe 145. Twinkie 146.
SCUM Manifesto 147. Sip-in 148. Barney Frank 149.
Don't Ask, Don't Tell 150. Conversion therapy 151. Gen-
esis 19:1–11 152. Castro Street 153. Pussy 154. Indigo Girls
155. *The Price of Salt* 156. Diesel-dyke 157. "Paul's Case"
158. Bisexual lesbian 159. Freddy Mercury 160. Opium

dens 161. *The History of Sexuality* 162. *Bowers v Hardwick* 163. Bathhouse 164. Sexual orientation 165. Straight 166. Compulsory heterosexuality 167. Transphobic 168. Homophobic 169. Cellular closet 170. *The Boys in the Band* 171. John Waters 172. Mom/Moms 173. John Gielgud 174. Open relationship 175. Adrienne Rich 176. *Giovanni's Room* 177. Cisgender 178. Faux queen 179. *Ei/Em/Eir* 180. Joan Jett 181. Diva 182. Falsies 183. *Glee*: "Blame It on the Alcohol" 184. Michel Foucault 185. Breeder 186. *Queer as Folk* 187. Barbara Stanwyck 188. Andy Warhol 189. Djuna Barnes 190. Gender identity disorder 191. Defense of Marriage Act 192. Pulse nightclub 193. Poofter 194. Keith Haring 195. Judy Chicago 196. Hate crime 197. Liberace 198. Openly gay 199. Ma Rainey 200. Limp-wrist 201. Neutrios 202. One earring 203. Flannel shirt 204. Herstory 205. *Paris Is Burning* 206. Leatherman 207. *Women's Barracks* 208. Ze/Hir/Hirs 209. Bicurious 210. Lesbian until graduation 211. Roland Barthes 212. Rainbow flag 213. Gaydar 214. *One, Inc* 215. Transvestite 216. Two-spirit 217. Henry James 218. Anna Freud 219. GLAAD 220. Gay-Straight Alliance 221. Ally 222. *Notes of a Crocodile* 223. Overcompensating 224. Lady boy 225. Johanna Metzger 226. Fat dick 227. *Close to the Knives: A Memoir of Disintegration* 228. Libertine 229. Bi questioning 230. Grindr 231. LGBTQ friendly 232. Trannyshack 233. Heteronormativity 234. Institutional oppression 235. Summer Taylor 236. Transgender hormone therapy 237. Transition 238. Gender neutral pronouns 239. Versatile 240. The Magnetic Fields 241. Pedro Almodóvar 242. Effeminate 243. Romantic orientation 244. *Sailor Moon* 245. Sex confirmation surgery 246. Trans-exclusionary radical feminist 247. Gay gene 248. E. M. Forster 249. Judy Garland 250. Kinsey Scale 251. *Naughty Bits* 252. Agender 253. Seme and uke

254. *The Intermediate Sex* 255. Embodiment theory 256. Keith Haring 257. Androphelia 258. Top surgery 259. Family Research Council 260. Vita Sackville-West 261. Susan Sontag 262. Melissa Etheridge 263. Dropping hairpins 264. Gay liberation movement 265. Radical Faeries 266. *Maurice* 267. *Symposium* 268. Károly Mária Kertbeny 269. Third gender 270. Eve Kosofsky Sedgewick 271. Virginia Woolf 272. Submissive 273. *Words of a Woman Who Breathes Fire* 274. Ricky Martin 275. Hijra 276. Gynephilia 277. "Notes on 'Camp'" 278. Doggy style 279. *Confessions of a Mask* 280. Bugger 281. Gay mafia 282. Fence sitter 283. Bloomsbury Group 284. Gay Liberation Front 285. Diane Fuss 286. Deviant 287. Bent 288. Hand job 289. *Blue Is the Warmest Color* 290. *Tales of the City* 291. Princess Diana 292. Army boots 293. Fetish 294. Paul Monette 295. Tiresias 296. *Jules et Jim* 297. Countee Cullen 298. Swish 299. *Dhalgren* 300. *Orlando* 301. Missionary position 302. International Gay and Lesbian Human Rights Commission 303. Carson McCullers 304. Neulisa Luciano Ruiz 305. Marilyn Hacker 306. *The Autobiography of Alice B. Toklas* 307. Sadie Lee 308. Closet queens 309. "Refugees from Amerika: A Gay Manifesto" 310. Gouine 311. Sarah Bernhardt 312. Hermaphroditus 313. *A Room of One's Own* 314. Tribadism 315. Hole 316. Diane Arbus 317. Lesbian Herstory Archives 318. Radicalesbians 319. Big dick 320. John Cheever 321. Penis envy 322. Neurotic 323. Isadora Duncan 324. Monika Diamond 325. Shaki Peters 326. Benjamin Britten 327. Billie Jean King 328. Amazons 329. Great American Lesbian Art Show 330. bell hooks 331. *The Four Witches* 332. Natalie Clifford Barney 333. Jane Bowles 334. H. D. 335. Erotic education 336. *While England Sleeps* 337. Oneida Community 338. Sixty-nine 339. *Sodometries* 340. *The Rocky Horror Picture Show* 341.

Sylvia Rivera 342. Wallace Thurman 343. Anal sex 344.
Frida Kahlo 345. *Studies in the Psychology of Sex* 346.
Codpiece 347. Pervy 348. Ménage à trois 349. Bury your
gays 350. Self-erasure 351. Joan Crawford 352. Dimorphic
353. Cunnilingus 354. Conversion narrative 355. *The Lad-
der* 356. Richard von Krafft-Ebing 357. Jeanette Winter-
son 358. Kate Millett 359. Lexi 360. Nina Pop 361.
Twilight Zone: "In His Image" 362. *Dykes to Watch Out
For* 363. Kitty Tsui 364. Bambis 365. Lytton Strachey
366. *Joy of Lesbian Sex* 367. *Funny Boy* 368. Zoning text
amendment 369. *Stone Butch Blues* 370. *A Boy's Own
Story* 371. Leatherdyke 372. Edward Albee 373. Edna St.
Vincent Millay 374. Polyandry 375. Anal play 376. David
M. Halperin 377. Hypothalamus 378. Harlem Renais-
sance 379. Oliver Sachs 380. Red bowtie 381. *Nightwood*
382. Gay sailor 383. *Sexual Behavior in the Human Male*
384. Undercut 385. Bluestocking Bookstore 386. Lesbian
vest 387. *Sodometries* 388. Swinging 389. Intimacy 390.
Bisexual chic 391. Spinster 392. *Blackbird* 393. *The Well of
Loneliness* 394. Oedipus complex 395. Finger-fucking
396. Dan Cameron 397. *Interview with a Vampire* 398.
Nancy Fried 399. "Relax" 400. Alexander McQueen 401.
Star Trek Next Generation: "The Outcast" 402. David
Bowie 403. Serena Angelique Velázquez Ramos 404.
Gore Vidal 405. Tony Kushner 406. Edmund White
407. Martina Navratilova 408. GenderPAC 409. Qiu
Miaojin 410. Coccinelle 411. *Rubyfruit Jungle* 412. *Love
Boat*: "Gopher's Roommate" 413. Pride march 414. Bryan
"Egypt" Powers 415. *Three Essays on the Theory of Sexual-
ity* 416. Queer Nation 417. Stealth bisexual 418. Sir Roger
Casement 419. Lavender Menace 420. Vanilla dykes 421.
The Little Review 422. Labrys 423. Bree Black 424. Fist-
ing 425. Smut 426. Sonnet 13 427. Ice pick lobotomy
428. Gay bashing 429. Kenneth Lewes 430. Chest har-

ness 431. Barebacking 432. Patricia Nell Warren 433. Chicken hawk 434. *The Homosexual in America: A Subjective Approach* 435. The Furies Collective 436. Rita Mae Brown 437. Carl Jung 438. Marriage equality 439. AIDS memorial quilt 440. Normals 441. Lesbian kiss episode 442. Friends: "The One with the Lesbian Wedding" 443. Anti-sodomy laws 444. Andy Bell 445. Leonard Bernstein 446. Chubby chaser 447. PrEP 448. *Obergefell v. Hodges* 449. Metrosexual 450. *Edinburgh* 451. Pink Triangle 452. Leather chaps 453. Dykes on Bikes 454. Nella Larson 455. Tennessee Williams 456. Lesbian Avengers 457. **Wimmen's** *Comix* 458. Jeremy Thorpe 459. Double-identity 460. Gay lisp 461. *The City and the Pillar* 462. *Ma vie en rose* 463. Samuel R. Delany 464. Androgyny 465. Lypsinka 466. Deep throating 467. *One Hundred Years of Homosexuality* 468. Gay panic defense 469. Pompadour 470. *Black Diaries* 471. We'wha 472. Colette 473. Lesbos 474. Frankie Goes to Hollywood 475. Masturbation 476. Monogamous 477. Fluffer 478. Pet Shop Boys 479. AZT 480. Valerie Solanas 481. **N**arcissus 482. Pedro Lemebel 483. Female impersonator 484. Eileen Myles 485. Larry Duplechan 486. Moral Majority 487. Sarah Schulman 488. Howard Cruse 489. Fop 490. Wank 491. Butt-fucker 492. She-man 493. Dominatrix 494. Vin Packer 495. Avatar 496. Édith Piaf 497. Flaming 498. Hustler 499. Pillow-biter 500. Monique Wittig 501 . . .

THEY FORMED ME. I WISH I HAD KNOWN.

Six Drawing Lessons

after William Kentridge's *Six Drawing Lessons*

1. In Praise of Shadows

This pressure for meaning, taking the fragments and completing an image, is present not only in this looking at shadows but in all that we see. Seeing here becomes a metaphor for all the images, and all the ways we apprehend the world.

I started drawing when I was around seven or eight. I wasn't doing well in my English classes. Art class was a refuge for me. I could focus on creating detailed and colorful images that my teachers almost always praised. More than that, drawing, like reading, sent me into a sort of fugue state. I didn't have to express myself verbally, and I could immerse myself and forget the world around me. Visual art was where my intelligence seemed most to manifest itself. On the other hand, when I tried to write a sentence, I felt an immediate spasm of fear, the sure knowledge I was getting everything wrong.

I trained as a visual artist all the way through college. My training was always intense, immersive, and probably preternaturally disciplined for a child my age. But, like a lot of individuals who train young in an art, at around twenty-two, after finishing art school, I decided that I had no real vision for myself as an artist. I generally tried to produce the work that was most likely to get me the approval of my current art teacher. One mentor told me that I worried too much about what he thought and gave me a B+ for that. The only B+, I think, that I ever received in an art class.

So, I gave up practicing art and went into arts administration, a path to a secure job and some sense of normalcy in my life. That's how I first encountered the South African artist William Kentridge. I was working as a fundraiser for the New Museum of Contemporary Art. His work was part of a group exhibition the museum was planning, and I needed to research his life, and production, for a grant proposal. I became consumed. Kentridge's art is, for one thing, deeply political, concerned with language, trauma, and social justice. What I admired about him was his level of technical ability and also the breadth of his craftmanship. He is a skilled draftsman—someone with the technical ability of Rembrandt—but he has never tethered himself to form. He is a printmaker. His experimental short films have revolutionized drawing and animation. He creates elaborate puppet shows that are produced by theaters around the world. But there's something deeper that drew me to him over many of the other brilliant artists whose work I fundraised for. The only way that I can put it is that his drawings and art are deeply articulate. The visual artists I've known have been among the most brilliant minds I've encountered, and also the least verbal. There is, when you look at Kentridge's work, a clear sense of the enormous intelligence of the person creating it. He is cogent about his process and as dedicated to documenting how he works as he is in presenting the work itself.

When I first came upon him, William Kentridge had built a solid reputation in South Africa but was still little known outside of his native country. The New Museum's principal curator, Dan Cameron, had dedicated himself, and the resources of the museum, to supporting outsider artists whose work confronted political realities, sometimes at the cost of the artist's personal safety. But that was the late '90s. Much has changed in Kentridge's career since, and he is now recognized among the preeminent visual artists of his generation.

The reason I'm interested in Kentridge, even now, is because, as a former visual artist trained in the classical mode, I've always been impressed by artists who develop a skill and then use that skill to master media and form. I also appreciate artists who explore and expose the why and how of what they do. If artists like Anselm Kiefer and Donald Judd are of late taking on heroic status, celebrated for their éclat, then Kentridge is antiheroic. His self-portraits, middle-aged, overweight, bejowled, erased, redrawn, erased—as if the artist can never quite find himself—practice a form of submission.

If you don't understand art, or have never worked the way Kentridge does, you'd be forgiven for thinking his work is messy. His signature drawing style is thick, gestural strokes made with charcoal and then erased to leave a smudge that is drawn over. Constant erasure is a no-no for most draftsmen: an indication that she is not seeing properly, that her eye is not connected to the hand, and the hand is not connected to the pen, and the pen is not connected to the page. But for Kentridge this erasure is an indication of process, of the real reason for putting charcoal to paper (as opposed, to say, taking a photograph). He rarely uses color, and when he does, it's a primary red, or blue, applied to make the viewer focus on a part of the drawing she might normally forget—or refuse—to see or to provide clarity. A self portrait of Kentridge standing, hands in pockets, as blue water slowly rises, the implication a drowning. Before I stopped drawing in my early twenties, that's how I liked to work. Large drawings, sometimes six feet to eight feet long, rendered in charcoal—thick black strokes that were rethought, erased, and then drawn over. "You can change charcoal," Kentridge offers in a recent interview, "as quickly as you can change your mind."

About a year ago, in the course of retraining myself how to draw, I discovered that Kentridge had published a series of lectures he'd given at Harvard called *Six Drawing Lessons*. I quickly located a used bookstore that had a copy available and arranged to have the book shipped to me. When the book arrived, I let it sit on the dining room table for six months. It was on top of a stack of junk that I always looked at. I didn't forget that it was there. But for some reason I couldn't pick it up to start reading.

The most likely reason is that it reminded me of the New Museum, a job that I had loved and the only job I've ever had that could be described as remotely glamorous. The other possibility is that back when I first encountered Kentridge, I believe I still had in my mind the possibility that I might return to being a visual artist. But now, here I was decades later—two decades that I had somehow let escape me—and there was something so off-putting about a book on art so densely dedicated to practice and that so clearly demonstrated Kentridge's mastery, a mastery gained from dedication, over time. Perhaps what I really wanted when I bought the book was some magic balm that would help make up for the twenty-five plus years that I *hadn't* practiced a craft.

When I did finally start reading, I found the book to be miraculous.

Kentridge begins by describing the creation of his experimental film *Shadow Processions*. According to Kentridge, the film is an animation of Plato's "Allegory of the Cave." For this animation, Kentridge created paper puppets, jointed with wire, and animated frame by frame under a camera. This is meant to mimic a process, common in puppet theater, of using flat cutouts and silhouetting them behind a screen or casting their shadows onto a screen. The characters processing include miners, a man and woman walking while reading aloud from what appears to be the Bible, a child, a hobbled soldier on crutches, a man carrying a broken city, an elderly man being transported in a wheelbarrow. According to Kentridge, this is the inventory of people he has met, or read about in the news, during his lifetime in Johannesburg.

For Kentridge, shadows are political. The people trapped in Plato's cave, and the people "trapped" in Kentridge's film, do not realize their condition. They believe they are experiencing reality. Kentridge agrees with Plato that it's the moral duty of the person who has seen the "light" to go back into the cave and release those who misperceive, but he simultaneously resists the absolute rightness of Plato's imperative. "The light at the end of the tunnel," Kentridge declares, "turns too quickly into the interrogator's spotlight."

Kentridge doesn't overtly state this, but I also wonder if the other reason that he begins his first drawing lesson with shadows is because, for anyone that trains as an artist, this is the first lesson—the one that, in the Western classical art tradition, distinguishes those who can't draw from those who can. Very young children, unless they're precocious, do not draw shadows. Even young children who are capable of fairly meticulous renderings don't include shadows. In fact, young children at around the age of six need to be taught about the existence of shadows—part science experiment, part art exercise. Even after being taught, most children don't include shadows because most children draw from memory not from life. We forget, it seems, the existence of shadows. If children do include shadows, it's not to create verisimilitude but because they've absorbed the meaning of shadow as something negative, as a symbol of unease.

Well, most of the time. I remember the first shadow I ever drew. When I was seven or eight, my teacher had my class sit one by one in front of a bright light and she, or a student helper, traced our profiles on a black sheet of paper and then helped us cut them out. I recall this because I was awed. The teacher displayed our artwork in a window, and I was mesmerized by the elegant beauty of it, the sunlight streaming from behind the cutouts. The word *silhouette,* which in its softness and it elongated *o* sounded nothing like any of the other English words I was learning. I had certainly seen plenty of photographs by then, but I imagine that was the first moment that I'd seen myself crafted. Kentridge relates a similar experience. He is seven years old, on a beach, and enamored with the ability to control the shape, and the dexterity and agility of this presence emanating from him alone.

I have to admit my first time through lesson one, I was a little disappointed. Kentridge is prone to statements that most of us learn in Introductory Aesthetics. Lines like: "When we say there is a horse, we mean there is something on the paper which triggers the recognition of HORSE in us." But, I keep reading because, despite the facileness of some of Kentridge's initial observations, they are always followed by an incisive, many times revelatory immersion in the artistic process. Take this passage that follows the sentence above:

> Ask someone to make a drawing of a horse rearing on its hind legs, and it is not easy (if you are not Delacroix). How far under the rump are the hooves? What is the angle between the mandible and the wing of the atlas? What is the relationship of the withers to the crest and the shoulder of the horse?

He ends by describing how the small scraps of black paper he has been shuffling around the page can be arranged in such a way as to resemble a horse, because in the blackness, in the simplified rendering, we can *only* see a horse rearing. "The pressure for meaning, taking the fragments and completing an image, is present not only in this looking at shadows but in all that we see."

Anyone who draws knows the truth of what Kentridge is describing. If you train long enough, you can become adept enough to reproduce without having to re-see it. But, that level of ability is rare. Most of us have to find someone who will stand in a certain posture or recreate from a photograph. For my cartoons I often end up staging elaborate tableaus that I photograph or have a friend help me photograph (if I need to be in the shot). Alison Bechdel uses a similar process. As much time as I have spent with my niece, as much as I love her, I cannot render her face without actually seeing a photograph of her. Kentridge is right, of course, sometimes the simplest gesture, the fragment, is more powerful. The more information we provide the more we walk that tenuous line of "getting it wrong."

But, of course, it's not that way with words. I have a bountiful reservoir of words that I can use to describe my niece. She never has to spend a moment in front of me for me to render her. And yet, what are words but etchings, dark gestures onto the page. Kentridge, later in lesson one, describes a typewriter as "a projector of the written word." For Kentridge, as is the case for most visual artists, words are not vessels of meaning (alone) but images in and of themselves. They depend, like any other visual image, on the illusion of representation.

About here in my rereading of Kentridge's first lesson is the place I feel the need to come up for air. It occurs to me, as I read, that I don't entirely know why I've engaged this text. I wonder why I need a middle-aged, white, heterosexual, cisgender man rooting around in my head. I've spent the better part of three decades trying to escape *that* voice. I'm firmly middle-aged, and by now I should be very good at what I do. I *am* most days the teacher. If I need to be instructed, it's because what I'm doing is really only a hobby, something I never plan to do with any seriousness or hope for accomplishment and recognition.

If I think, however, of the now nearly lost denotation of lesson, a passage of scripture read during a religious service, the word of God delivered by man, I recognize that being constantly taught is a component of discipline. It's not, after all, as if after a half century of churchgoing, a parishioner can get up from the pew, walk out, and come back when the reading is over. It's part of the practice of faith, an act of humbling oneself, to remain even when you've heard the words many times before.

2. A Brief History of Colonial Revolts

This is not old history. It is where we still are embedded, in questions surrounding drone attacks in Afghanistan or Médicins Sans Frontières (Doctors without Borders) in Somalia. The Herero genocide is part of a continuing set of questions and actions, questions of seeing, understanding, and the use of violence, a set of questions reaching from Plato's cave to where we are here, and the studio becomes an emblematic space for working these questions.

I came of artistic age in North Carolina during the Andres Serrano "Piss Christ" and Robert Mapplethorpe controversy. Senator Jesse Helms made repeated attacks against the artists and the National Endowment for the Arts for providing support to the institutions exhibiting these artists' work. I'm certain I didn't see any Mapplethorpe images other than his phallic Calla lilly and I had a mature enough aesthetic, even in high school, to know that Serrano's "Piss Christ" was, actually, a beautiful image. I sympathized deeply with the attacked artists and probably imagined myself, dressed in all black, purple-haired, as someone equally worthy of attack. I was horrified then to receive a handwritten note of congratulations from Helms when I won a silver key for one of my own photographs in the National Scholastic Arts Competition. I handed the letter to my mother and scoffed and she chastised me for not showing enough respect. I still find Helms' attacks on Serrano and Mapplethorpe deeply reprehensible, but he is also, still, the only politician who has ever written me anything, much less anything kind.

The truth is, in America at least, time takes the bite out of political art. Serrano has never been clear if the crucifix in his photograph is actually suspended in piss, and he is certainly not the first artist to incorporate viscera in his work. Compared to, say the performance artists Paul McCarthy and Vito Acconci, Serrano's glowing, pristine images are off-putting if you expend a lot of brain power imagining urine instead of actually looking. Robert Mapplethorpe was a solid studio portrait photographer, but I'm not convinced he was a great one. His compositions aren't particularly inspired, and there's little attention to psychological acuity. Compare Mapplethorpe to the great Diane Arbus or even Sally Mann. I've also found Mapplethorpe's objectification of the queer black male body to be problematic.

With the rise and the mainstreaming of queer culture, his images have certainly begun to lose their ability to shock. There's a Robert Mapplethorpe print—two naked men, arms and legs entwined—hanging in my hairdresser's studio. I've watched numerous Philadelphia moms sit under the poster and prattle away. If they even notice the Mapplethorpe, I doubt any one of them imagine it causing anyone any pain anywhere, ever. Even the truly great political artist of the '80s and '90s,

David Wojnarowicz, doesn't shock us as he once did. I asked my students recently what they thought of the graphic gay sex scenes in *Close to the Knives*. They shrugged. They'd seen that stuff on the internet, they told me.

To be a political artist in America is to engage in fisticuffs in the carnival rather than to really stand and oppose an oppressive regime. I don't doubt that we have barely perceived the destruction Trump has wrought, but it's also true that the worst thing that will happen to us, and by us I mean those of us lucky enough to be middle class enough to have an artistic practice—is that we will have the Whitney unceremoniously—or perhaps ceremoniously since the spectacle is sure to make its way to Instagram—take down our work in the middle of its biennial and ship it, carefully and archivally crated, back to our studio. Not one of us will be disappeared in the night, our family left to learn what happened to our body decades later when our case file is opened by a truth and reconciliation tribunal. Outside of the great queer visual artists who came out of the AIDS crisis—most of whom *are* dead and *were* abandoned very openly by the institutions that could have saved them—and a handful of black and brown and queer artists—Kara Walker and Faith Ringgold comes to mind—there are surprisingly few visual artists who make it to the top echelons of our larger cultural imagination who actively, incisively, and effectively take on the evils of American history with scalpel in hand. (This is, to be fair, at least in part due to the effectiveness of Jesse Helms' attacks on the NEA and the resulting timidity that it inspired in mainstream institutions that support the arts and artists.)

The world's great political visual artists then, and I do acknowledge that this is arguable, come from outside the United States. William Kentridge might be the preeminent among them. William Kentridge has for over four decades maintained a constant, unwavering, consistently excellent, and politically conscious artistic practice, even at times of great social upheaval.

That's an extraordinary feat of mental and physical prowess, particularly when you consider how he works and what he makes art about.

But this status can also be deemed problematic. The art critic Alan Gilbert put it this way when I asked him about Kentridge's importance: "I'm one of the rare people who doesn't seem to be a fan. To begin with, I've always found it troubling that the most famous artist from the African continent is white (and from a privileged background). Although of course I'm not surprised. And while he's been described as a critic of Apartheid and racial inequity, I've always found his work a bit tame in that regard, although I'm guessing I've maybe missed some of that since it might be shown less here in the United States . . . I've always wanted it to do just a little more."

Kentridge's second lesson begins with a letter written in 1915 by John Chilembwe, a very successful Baptist preacher and the founder of the Providence Industrial Mission, a church in what was then called Nyasaland, and is now Malawi. Chilembwe's letter to the *Nyasaland Times* is three paragraphs long, and Kentridge includes the entire text. In essence, Chilembwe asks a concession from the British government: if the British wanted Black Africans to fight and die in their armies then the colonizer should recognize the basic humanity of the black man. He isn't asking for an independent state, simply that the Natives—as he refers to his countrymen and himself—be accorded dignity.

According to Kentridge, the letter was never published and Chilembwe led a revolt. The British crushed the rebellion, executed Chilembwe, and dynamited his church. The British made postcards from photographs of the ruins and distributed those postcards throughout the British colonies. Kentridge tells us that he tried to make a feature film from the incident that was never produced (correctly, Kentridge informs us): "I think I was impelled to make the film from two postcards, the church intact and a church in ruins, and by the broad logic of colonial-

ism providing its own critique, the language of the Enlightenment used to criticize its own institutions, in Rawlsian terms,
of justice as fairness." Kentridge goes on to add that a copy of
the letter is stashed in a desk drawer in his studio.

Reproductions of the postcards are provided us on the following page. The first is of a solid brick structure, large, with
a basilica and side chapels. A caption reads, "Chelemawi's
Church, Nyasaland, No 1." The next postcard is of a cloud of
dust, only the shadow of trees can be discerned. The caption
reads "Chelemawi's Church, Nyasaland, No 5." The final photograph reveals a pile of rubble covered by what looks like a
giant, broken leaf but is actually the pitched roof of the church.
One spire still stands. The caption for this postcard reads, "Chelemawi's Church, Nyasaland, No 8." It's the numbering that gets
to me the most, the blanks exposed by what's missing. I tried to
find images of the postcards using a Google search, but I was
never able to determine if there was a postcard 2, 3, 4, 6, and 7.
I don't know why they bother me so much—these postcards—
other than that I hadn't comprehended that a people would
make *cards* out of such misery and destruction. Kentridge himself never makes a comment on the postcards themselves—
beyond clearly recognizing their horror.

The lesson goes on to connect the battle of Waterburg in
1904, Mozart's *Magic Flute,* a production of *Magic Flute* in Ber-
lin in 1938, his own production of Mozart's *Magic Flute,* his
studio process, the invention and reinvention of Africa, a Johannesburg social studies class in 1963 during which he was made
to watch films about the superiority of white culture to Xhosa
culture, the Hottentot Venus, and Picasso in Paris making
"African" masks. Kentridge links all these seemingly disparate
concepts by pointing out their connection to Enlightenment
thought. "It is not that every act of violence has had its public relations, its brochures, its paintings and murals of a better
life. But rather, and more difficult to apprehend, is that every

act of enlightenment, all the missions to save souls, all the best impulses, are so dogged by the weight of what follows them: their shadow, the violence that accompanies enlightenment."

Throughout his exploration he apologizes for the fragmented associations he makes. "I feel strongly the lack of clarity, the jumping from subject to subject in my talk, and the shift between wanting to make it smoother, to make more elegant connections." I'm confused by the act of effacement. To me the lesson is brilliant. The lecture reminds me of his work: quick, assured gestures and the humbling, the erasures. I keep reading and re-reading to determine if he is indeed being humble, or if he's being disingenuous. And then I wonder if his lecture isn't something else altogether—a practice in a kind of technique all itself.

Kentridge has developed over the past two decades a process for creating drawings that he refers to as *fortuna*. Its genesis appears to be in surrealist and Dadaist automatism that was meant to tap the artist's subconscious to reveal the truths of the psyche. Automatism was always a performative act. The point was in the process of making oneself vulnerable to what was hidden within—not the final result. But unlike automism, which relied on random movements and gestures, Kentridge describes fortuna as "something outside the range of cold statistical chance and, something too, outside the range of rational control." It's something akin, according to Kentridge, to listening to someone speak. When speaking naturally a person will draw on available language, cultural markers, and personality tics to reveal who they really are. What's revealed should be unconsidered.

There's something startling to me about this idea. That one should make political art out of the subliminal. Political art with its genesis in rhetoric and the polemical should be carefully considered to ensure one is on the right side, whatever that side might be. Language should be burnished or polished lest someone question your loyalty or worse cancel you. I rarely post on Twitter not out of high-mindedness but out of fear of what one poorly worded statement might do to my career. But Kentridge is clear: when we go into the studio we should be willing to get our hands dirty.

I've always seen, needed to see, my life as a carefully thought out and worded narrative. The idea of making myself vulnerable fills me with a sort of fear. It's not political correctness or a fear of liberalism. It's a fear of what I will reveal about myself, the prejudices and conceits I don't want to acknowledge. I had come to Kentridge believing that I would find answers on how to find an artistic practice and what I find, instead, is a deep critique of the privilege of being able to utter those questions at all. You have an artistic practice to stand as a monument to the failures of history as writ across your body, your life, your thoughts.

3. Vertical Thinking

Charcoal and paper are not perfect substances. Charcoal can be erased easily, but not perfectly. The paper is tough and can be erased, redrawn, erased, and still hold its structure— but not without showing its damage. The erasure is never perfect. A gray smudge of charcoal dust lodged in the paper fibers remains as the ghost of the image before its alteration.

For a city that I've spent at most 48 hours in, Johannesburg has taken up an extraordinary slice of my imagination. I grew up during the apex of the anti-Apartheid movement and knew what Soweto was before I knew of Cabrini Green, Eight Mile Road, Oakland, Far Rockaway. As a teenager, I joined Amnesty International (really run by the CIA, my mother knowingly informed me) and hung their posters of raised fists behind barbed wire on my bedroom wall. I sang the lyrics of "Biko" with passion. In college I joined the anti-Apartheid protests and unknowingly, and very momentarily, joined the communist party as well. *That* came up during my citizenship test a year later.

What can I say? I was young.

To be fair to my youthful self, my life at the time was very divided and, looking back, I feel like I barely lived in the American South. I had no familial attachment to it and despised the racial politics. My connections were to Sri Lanka and to England. When I traveled to England my family—all of whom are Sri Lankan—referred to themselves as Blacks and saw themselves as part of a larger fight. In America, I existed in some strange neverland of not actually, or even remotely wanting to be, thought of as white and certainly not a victim of the continual and relentless racial oppression suffered by African Americans or a part of the vibrant and rich culture that had arisen as a response. In my senior year of college, I won a grant from the Documentary Center at Duke University for a photo essay on growing up Asian in the American South. After my presentation, one of the attendees, an African American woman, thanked me and said that the presentation surprised her. She had thought that Asians identified as white, and she appreciated that I had chosen not to. I didn't deserve congratulations, but I may not have made that decision if not for my awareness of British and South African racial politics.

My forty-eight hours in Johannesburg was my first moment in South Africa, a country I had long wanted to visit. I was really only passing through Johannesburg on my way to the Transkei and, in my jet-lagged haze, I remember only three things. The first, and most salient, is the golden hills, which are not made of gold but actually of toxic mining waste called tailings. These hills glisten white in the sun and look not at all this earth. They are artificial constructions, standing as a testament to a terrible history. They also separate the main city—once mostly white but now very integrated—from the townships—still mostly black and very poor. My second memory is of the Maboneng Precinct where I stayed. I fell in love with the neighborhood, which was mostly Black, and vibrant for it, with murals and high-end restaurants and a thriving artistic culture. It was progressive, dynamic, first world. It reminded me of what North Philadelphia might actually look like if its various local, state, and national governments ever thought to care for the infrastructure and the people. The last memory is of a moment in the Apartheid Museum. My friend and I were passing a group of Black schoolchildren—they looked to be nine or ten—when one of them gleefully yelled at my friend, "P. W. Botha." My friend was taken aback and muttered a *what*. The child grinned and turned away. My friend looked viscerally pained though he never said anything about the taunt.

I found the boy ten minutes later in another part of the museum. I asked him what he thought of the museum, if he thought it had anything to do with his life now. He laughed, "Ma'am, I don't understand you." He narrowed his eyes at me, "I don't speak English." That, I suspect, was a lie. But he knew I was a foreigner. I had no authority over him or the world we were standing in, and he wasn't going to speak to me ever. But why I really remember this is because, "I don't speak English," has been a retort I've been tempted to try on many occasions as a response to the busybody questions of well-meaning strangers. I've wanted it to act as a restatement and recapitulation of the racism I suspect most people harbor. But I've never had the moxie to actually utter that in the presence of someone else. I was impressed by this ten-year-old's willingness to put me in my place.

I mention all this because Kentridge's third drawing lesson is about Johannesburg and about the way place informs—actually creates—artistic practice. The physical landscape of

Johannesburg is the result of a meteor strike the force of which pushed up the hills for which Johannesburg is famous and created the Witwatersrand basin. That meteor strike also created, or exposed, the richest gold deposits in the world. Johannesburg, Kentridge tells us in his lecture, is unusual for a large city. It is not founded beside or around a geographical entity such as a river, an ocean, a piedmont, a delta. Instead, Johannesburg sits on top of gold. About halfway through the lecture, Kentridge shows us a surveyor's map of Johannesburg. Because it's a surveyor's map, it's a record not just of what Johannesburg was at the time (Kentridge informs us that about three percent of the streets and buildings in the map actually existed) but of what Johannesburg would be one day. Today, 120 years after the drawing of this map, almost all of that original "virtual" city exists. Kentridge goes on to add: "In the way that a drawing is a membrane between the world coming toward us, a negotiation between ourselves and that which is outside, this map becomes an emblematic drawing . . ."

When I read this, I think of Kentridge's charcoal self-portraits: drawn, erased, rebuilt. Kentridge informs us that he started drawing around nine, and that he started at that age drawing landscapes. Through the process of his art education, he realized that the landscapes he built along a horizon—what you're taught when you learn three-point perspective—was actually something else. Classical perspective was useless in capturing the truth of what Kentridge was sitting on, and instead he needed to think of the city he loved vertically.

When I read this, something clicks for me about Kentridge's process. Because Kentridge came to prominence outside of South Africa fairly late in his life—when he was in his mid-forties—it's hard to find images of him when he *wasn't* middle-aged. And his renderings of himself are brutal. These aren't the wizened and sly self-portraits of Rembrandt posing in Masonic regalia. Kentridge's self-portraits are vulnerable. For example, the series of standing full nudes drawn from behind. This has to be almost unheard of in self-portraits—a portrait of the back. But there is Kentridge, naked, head to toe, overweight and flabby. He's presenting himself as the subject of the viewer's erotic gaze, but he doesn't even bother to fudge a little, place a shadow here or there that might define muscle. No dad bod for him. If you know something of the history of the objectification of the female and black body, then these self-portraits are, in their honesty, and frank humor, about aging men, strangely satisfying.

Or there's the Benefactor in his animation "Monument." The Benefactor, glutinous, overbearing, repulsive, if you look closely, is Kentridge himself. These portrayals don't seem entirely fair. Kentridge, for one thing, comes from a prominent Jewish family. He is very privileged, but he is also in South African society an outsider. His mother and father were both defense lawyers and often defended Black clients. His father represented the families of the protesters killed during the Sharpeville massacres. Kentridge mentions discovering, in his father's studio, the photographs of the brutalized bodies of Black men and women—though he doesn't valorize his father or the work his father did.

Of course, Kentridge isn't the first visual artist to visit history on his own body. Performance artists have been doing this for a half century now. The work of Marina Abramovic, Yoko Ono, Bob Flanagan, Chris Burden come to mind. And they all to varying painful degrees inflicted harm on themselves. Kentridge's drawings are sedate in comparison. And, yet, I still find Kentridge's willingness to mark and remark his own body in relation to South Africa's brutal history fascinating. Self-portraits are meant to demonstrate both skill and the ability to capture interiority. Kentridge's self-portraits—fleshy and brutish—are penance. They are vertical deconstructions of self as the price paid for history.

I respect him for offering his own body.

I wonder then what it means for me to think vertically about my own self. I realize my twenty-year-old mistake. I thought I had to prove skill. Now I realize that all I have to offer is my body. My body as presence, as protest, as historical mistake. A cervix and womb that is now surely useless and collapsing. A body once imagined, that came to take up space, and now in middle age is slowly relinquishing it. A body marked and scarred and erased and etched back. A threadbare body, patched and re-patched. I've never appreciated when my teachers made grandiose pronouncements about what is needed to make great art so I'm not going to utter what seems to come next. That to be an artist I need to draw myself debased. But I do think that decades ago I gave up because I thought far too highly of myself. Now, I see myself as small in the vastness of whatever it is that unfurls before me: culture, history, time. I have never been very much at all and now why not keep at what little I have.

4. Practical Epistemology

In the studio, I film my eight-year-old son. He takes a jar of paint and a handful of pencils, some books and papers. He throws the jar of paint across the studio walls, scatters the pencils, tears the papers and scatters the shards. We run the film in reverse. There is a utopian perfection. The papers reconstruct themselves every time. He gathers them all. He catches twelve pencils, all arriving from different corners of the room in the same moment. In the jar he catches all the paint—not a drop spilled. The wall is pristine.

Drawing is, I believe, the only art form that everyone, across cultures, has practiced at some point in their lives. Every child draws—even if they eventually give up the practice and move on. I tell my cartooning students that I hate the term *illiterate*.

It privileges only one kind of literacy—the verbal sort. It interests me how many immigrant cartoonists mention that their love of cartoons and comics developed at a young age because comics, along with television, was how they first felt most comfortable engaging with the English language. I had a similar experience.

But despite our intrinsic visual fluency, and despite our nearly universal experience as draftsmen, most people forget how physical drawing actually is. We stand—or sit on a stool—for two main reasons. So that we can engage our whole bodies in the production of what we're doing and because standing is the best way to position ourselves in space in order to judge perspective. When you sit down, you began to collapse into yourself and you begin to limit the range and fluidity of your body and to limit the range and fluidity of your work.

To be a visual artist, then, is also to know how to navigate and order space. I always enjoyed life drawing class the most. The majority of us, when we are asked to draw a hand, draw our everyday perspective of a hand: from the top, five fingers, spread out, nails fully visible. But that isn't how our hand looks in space and, to learn to really draw, you have to override what your cerebral cortex is insisting—that this is a hand that is made of five fingers, and nails, and a palm—and see a hand is space, which depending on your viewpoint and angle could mean missing a finger, without nails, be almost all knuckle, no visible wrist. In drawing class, you learn not to see with words but to see shapes, and this necessitates giving up the knowledge you've learned for the knowledge you're gaining in the moment. One of my favorite artists is John Singer Sargent. My love for him has been longstanding and I've held on to it even when teachers (and artist friends) scoffed at my lowbrow taste. He's had a recent resurgence largely because of the recognition among art historians and critics that Sargent was likely gay. I've read a few art critics who have suggested that the visceral energy of his portraits come from his feeling of outsider-ness and his empathy for other outsiders: his Jewish patrons, women, brown and Black men and women. I am very willing to believe this, but I also think his brilliance stems from a very simple fact. Sargent spent his life training himself to *observe*, to comprehend what existed in space and time and not what language or culture told him to see.

Drawing, because it's performative also teaches you what it means to be uncomfortable in space. Almost all the visual artists I know complain now of some sort of physical ailment from a life of heavy lifting, standing, slouching over drafting tables. I learned young to override my body's signals of discomfort so I could stand for hours painting. In that sense, I think drawing is more akin to dancing. I was recently on a long flight with a friend who had trained as a dancer up until her twenties. I looked over at one point and noticed she had folded herself carefully in her seat, delicate as origami, and she hadn't moved for hours. "Aren't you uncomfortable?" I asked. She gave me the side eye and then admitted that she hadn't thought about it until I said something. "I was a ballet dancer. I spent my youth learning to ignore my body's discomfort," she mused, before closing her eyes to take a nap.

I mention all this because Kentridge's fourth lesson is really about the body in art. He informs that he's moved us from the shadows in Plato's cave, to the Enlightenment and the colonial history of Africa, to Johannesburg, to his studio. This is, of course, a demonstration of vertical thinking and it also resembles, as many of you have probably already guessed, the focusing of a camera. And much of Kentridge's lesson is dedicated to the relationship between the body and space, seeing, and the medium.

For Kentridge, the making of visual art is about releasing and then controlling the body, about, as he puts it, "trusting the physical." "We look at something usually taken for granted," he tells us, "the passage of time, the movement of a person, and in the studio we demand its reconstruction, its shattering. Time changed into marked graduations of animation: learning its grammar in hope that in the end something different will emerge."

Kentridge uses this term *grammar* many times in the lesson, and I hadn't actually heard that term applied to visual arts until fairly recently. I was struggling through a graphic essay, and I sent the page proofs to a friend of mine who is a visual artist. I told him that I kept seeing all my mistakes. He wrote me back, "No, no. Stop. Embrace the mistakes and let them become the internal grammar of the piece, and eventually your style." Up to that point, grammar had felt a bludgeon. I started to draw because I could barely master English grammar. As a writing instructor I was taught that I must fix and help my students standardize their grammar. My friend, and now Kentridge, were offering me a different possibility. Skill resulted not from the mastery of an accepted grammar but in the ability to use a medium to establish something unpredictable and original but also simultaneously observed.

What I'm really acknowledging here is that Kentridge's practical epistemology is really about a nerdy love of process and of having fun. He breaks down a film camera, a stereoscope, a zoetrope, an etching press. He writes about filming himself walking backward and then reversing that film and realizing that simple reversal, him now walking forward, did not in fact look natural. This taught him that there's a natural grammar and intention to movement. He talks about turning his own body into a camera using a Claude glass. And above all he insists on the need for the artist to be playful . . . and stupid.

My favorite part of the lesson is the last page. Kentridge reminds us to make space for stupidity. "Understanding, hoping, believing, not out of conviction, but from physical experience, that from the physical making, from the very

imperfections of technique—our bad backward walking—
parts of the world, and parts of us, are revealed, that we neither
expressed nor knew, until we saw them." I spend a lot of class
time telling my students not to be afraid of being bad. Like a
lot of my teaching, it's my older self talking to my younger self,
saying what I wish someone had said to me. So, it's important
to me, exhilarating actually, to see a great artist—one of the
world's greatest political artists—reaffirm what I've long sus-
pected. That a very good training, a long practice, really should
make us aware of how very bad we are at whatever we're doing
and give us the confidence to embrace it and recognize that *this*
is also a source of originality.

5. In Praise of Mistranslation

The rhinoceros in the woodcut is covered with armored plating,
what appears to be rivets holding the plates of the armor together.
There is a secondary horn on the shoulder, like the small horn on
the breastplate of a horseman in a full suit of armor at a tourna-
ment. A scalloped plate on its hindquarters is both of fabric and a
metal skirt. But the eye looks forward, at odds with the hard cara-
pace with which the body is covered. The eye of the rhinoceros is
the punctum of the image, or the other, that which we are not.

I have always been terrible at spelling. I made terrible marks
on spelling tests, and I think the only thing that kept me from
being placed in remedial English classes was that I tested high
on the IQ tests that were routinely given to American school
children in the '70s and '80s. Part of the problem is that, when I
was young, I tried to spell English words the way they sounded,
which felt logical at the time. I still don't truly understand why
both *of* and *off* must exist. What cruel language insists there is a
meaningful difference between past and passed?

The second reason has to do with my father's library. My father had boxes and boxes of books carried with him from Sri Lanka to England. In England during the five years we lived there, my father compulsively bought books. He loved books but grew up very poor and had to borrow them from a school library. The first thing he started to do when he began to earn money was to acquire the library he could not afford as a child. And like many bibliophiles, he loaned me his favorite books, which I read avidly. It wasn't until junior high that one of my teachers—a Thomas Hardy lover, anglophile, and a frequent traveler to Great Britain—noticed that I was using the English spellings of words. She pointed it out to me. I still have to think for a moment. Is it *gray,* or *grey?*

In this lesson, Kentridge is interested in visual, as well as verbal, translations and mistranslations. He starts off with a discussion of asen, a type of ritual altar associated with East African vodun, and moves into rebuses and pictograms. What draws Kentridge to all these is that there is at the heart of them a riddle, and at the heart of every riddle is the possibility of an interesting error. Kentridge then moves toward what he regards as the overdetermined image: the image that invests in a heavily detailed account as a proof of its authenticity.

Many readers will recognize what Kentridge is describing in the passage I quoted at the beginning of this section. Albrecht Dürer's woodcut of a rhinoceros. This print is so famous that if you type Dürer into a Google search it will prompt you with "Dürer rhino." It's well known that Dürer had never seen a real rhinoceros and was basing his version on written accounts. Dürer draws on his imagination, and his version, bellicose, multi-horned and grotesque, reveals as much about Dürer as it does about any living rhinoceros. But, and this is important, Dürer doesn't believe he's guessing. He believes he has decoded correctly what a rhinoceros is. Kentridge also mentions Pietro Longhi's far more complicated 1751 rendering of Clara the rhinoceros (a real rhinoceros that was exhibited throughout Europe in the mid-1700s). Kentridge gives several interpretations of the riddle that this admittedly odd painting presents. The first he notes is that the image is possibly one of phallus and castration, since Clara's horn is missing and the rhino's horn has long been coded and decoded as a symbol of the male phallus. But, here, Kentridge is possibly making a mistake. Longhi is painting what he's seeing. For a time, Clara's horn did go missing. It was either removed to protect her handlers or she rubbed it off in the sort of self-mutilation often witnessed in wild animals held captive. Kentridge does acknowledge the terrible cost to the species of our human mistranslation of its horn. The rhino has been hunted to near extinction.

The rest of the lesson is an elegant meditation on the way misunderstanding leads to imagination. A child's misunderstanding of cat-flap (pet door in America) leads to a household pet growing wings and taking flight. The recognition that "der Vorhang der Pupille" in Rilke's "Der Panther" could be translated into English either *curtain,* as it typically is, or as *shutter*—transforming the panther into a type of camera.

As I reflect on the idea of translation and mistranslation I keep returning to Dürer's woodcut. Overdetermined is a criticism you hear a lot in a visual arts workshop. Most beginning artists create overdetermined work because beginners equate excess with skill. I remembered being shocked at my teacher's reactions when I first started drawing. The drawings that I put the most work in, that I labored over, drew and redrew were criticized for being overdetermined. But the drawings that were quick, often done in a few minutes without much thought, were lauded.

In art class, you learn very quickly that drawing something too realistically causes it at some point to lose its animating spark. And Kentridge is right—Dürer's desire to prove he knew what an animal he'd never seen looks like robs the image of looking like anything real. But, the thing is I've seen that rhino before. By that, I don't mean the actual woodcut, which I've seen many times. There's an echo of something else in my mind—it works its way into my consciousness like a musical earworm. And then it comes to me. The cartoonist and graphic designer Mœbius has drawn and redrawn Dürer's rhinoceros in his own fantastical work. And Mœbius's artwork is hugely influential on the art designers for George Lucas's original *Star Wars* trilogy. Dürer's "overdetermined" fantasy placed in its right context winds its way into our modern imaginations despite its errors.

There exists a problem with translation and mistranslation that Kentridge never acknowledges. Dürer created his rhinoceros from his own visual vocabulary and in doing so he mistranslated and created a fantastical animal. Our visual vocabularies are often riven with mischaracterizations and outright fallacies. One of the major problems, for example, with fantasy writing over the past half century is the way fantasy writers have unwittingly (or sometimes very purposefully) transmitted racialized imagery to an impressionable audience. The visual image impacts us far more vividly than the word and embeds itself far more surreptitiously. In absence we too often invite the grotesque. The problem with mistranslation as a generative exercise is that the "radically hollowed" image doesn't simply go poof but is filled instead with our biases and assumptions.

Which brings me to a mistranslation that has long bothered me. In my early thirties, a Buddhist monk told me that the Pali dukkha had been mistranslated by Western scholars. Western scholars of Buddhism, almost all of whom had been originally raised in the Judeo-Christian tradition translated the word into a common Christian concept, suffering. So, the four Noble truths are often translated as truths about suffering. The monk, however, told me that dukkha is far broader than suffering. It does imply pain but it's more accurate, but far less elegant, to translate into a sort of continual craving. "The hunger you feel when you've missed a meal" is how the monk put it. But, the monk also insisted, this hunger is never ceasing. The monk's explanation made me rethink my relationship to Buddhism, which had always been fraught (and still is). I'd never been able to reconcile the religion's insistence on our suffering. It felt to me like some bad country song, not true to the way I wanted to see my life. But the sensation of something slowly and persistently gnawing at me. That I understood, viscerally. Yet, as I write this I wonder if I'd been told the correct translation from the beginning if I would have cared as much. To get to the right meaning at the right time is an act that contains the power and impact of learning the meaning of the riddle, the power of initiation. I imagine that's what Kentridge is getting at in his lesson.

At the heart of the lesson is the ache for the visceral and the uncaptured: the need to let loose, to lose, to let the mind wind and unwind and the failure that comes about when one doesn't let that happen. Dürer focused too hard to prove all rhinoceros when he should have gone out searching for the one real thing. Longhi's painting, as bizarre as it is, and it is bizarre, is also far more accurate to the state of one particular rhino. And it comes to me that I have put for far too long faith in the page as some sort of proof—an overdetermined container of talent, intelligence, imagination—when all the energy was in my perpetual and constantly self-generating mistakes, my misperceptions, malapropisms, my misapprehensions, most of which precede me, will be what is judged, and most of which I have never been quite aware.

6. Anti-Entropy

The meaning is always a construction, a projection, not an edifice—something to be made, not simply found. There is always a radical incoherence and a radical instability. All certainties can only be held together by a text, a threat, an army, a fatwa, a sermon—that holds the fragments in an iron grip.

Kentridge doesn't in any of his lessons offer drawing prompts or exercises. He does suggest this: "What is the hope? That through the course of the last five lectures, there are images or thought that have remained, even in fragmented form. The invitation is to try to hold onto a narrative, or to construct a narrative . . ."

He tells us to shatter a vase in our studio and organize the fragments. He presents as an offering his lesson as fragments. I want to be a good student, and I've yet to create my own drawing. Here is my attempt at dark strokes on a white page:

In this essay:

I start making art because I can't speak.

I give up making art after fifteen years.

I read about Kentridge as part of my job.

I come back to art after twenty-five years.

I find Kentridge's *Six Drawing Lessons,* and I think maybe he can teach me to draw.

I'm interested in Kentridge because he is a political artist and I believe that gives heft to his work.

Kentridge is a hero, my hero.

When I finally work up the courage to open the book, Kentridge tells me, as I was always afraid he would, he doesn't have any interest in being a hero but he will hold an open studio.

I go to the open studio because I have always enjoyed those. I can touch the drawings when the artist turns away.

I remember while staring at the print of Dürer's woodcut that many of us say we don't like Dürer but his rhino inadvertently ends up in our artwork anyway.

(Rhino as the original photobomber?)

I add a few lines to Kentridge's drawing of a panther, lines that he will never know about.

I know that you're reading that and thinking that isn't an accurate drawing of the five essays that proceed this. But, if you go back and look you'll see I'm not entirely wrong. And you'll see the pattern because I'll insist that you must. That's the power of anti-entropy—of storytelling.

Kentridge begins the sixth lesson with the tale of Perseus as Kentridge's grandfather related the myth during a long train ride when Kentridge was a child. Kentridge is most shocked by the moment in the tale when Perseus sends the discus flying and kills the old beggar in the stands. As a child he's horrified at the randomness of that and as an adult it continues to haunt him. What if the old man had just been sitting one seat over? What if he had decided not to go at all? The randomness of it all. Entropy. From there he moves to the attempt in 19th century to synchronize all clocks and how Europe dictated those synchronized times to it colonies, creating a grid that resembles a bird cage, a kind of geography of time. The colonial rebellions, Kentridge notes correctly, were rebellions against this imposition of time.

My favorite part of the entire lesson comes right after his section describing his room of failures. It starts with the retelling of a Ghanaian proverb:

He that fled his fate, a journey of sixty years.

While he was going it waited for him—seated next to the gutter

Side:
And it said, 'Come let us eat,—my dear friend!'
And when he asked it, 'Who is it?'—it said, 'Am I
not thy fate?'

From there, Kentridge recasts Einstein's twin paradox. Two twins: one leaves and the other stays. One transforms into Odysseus on the journey. The other into an aged Odysseus, who has never left Ithaca, welcoming the youthful voyager home. There's the self and of course the shadow self. And then there are two Kentridges, one at Harvard and one still in Johannesburg, engaging in a Socratic discourse, and just as suddenly we're at the edge of a black hole, and then, finally, in the boat with Charon, examining the remnants that those entering Hades have left behind. It's a beautiful, thrilling spiral.

But I am also a bit annoyed, as I have been with all of my teachers, particularly the best ones. He hasn't given me anything I had wanted when I originally bought his books. There are no drawing exercises. He doesn't talk much about his charcoal technique. He definitely doesn't provide me with a blueprint for political art. Or, he does but the process—fragment, collage, re-fragment, collage—feels too open to misinterpretation. I wanted to see inside the meaning-making machine that creates exactitude and profundity.

But I've also been doing this long enough to recognize Kentridge's method. Like any good teacher, he is right to refuse to give me the answer. Any answer he gives would have been right, only for him, at some point in time long since passed. The twin encased in the rocket. He is right to insist that I use my hard-earned studio space and shatter my own vase. As I sit with the fragments, sliding and re-sliding them across the table, the cognitive illusion flips:

*

Twenty-five years ago, because I had been working hard, I needed to rest my eyes.

When I looked up at the studio clock, I realized over two decades had passed.

I reexamined the project I'd been working on and, now fully rested, recognized it.

I wrote at the bottom:

Bon à tirer

End drawing lesson six.

Punctum, Studium, and The Beatles' "A Day in the Life"

Dear V,

I'm ecstatic to hear from you, and I think it's your emails alone that sustain me these days. I know we barely know each other on some level, and, yet, it must mean something important if we're able to write at such length—or at least it shows we might actually be able to tolerate each other when we meet in person again. I hope.

You ask me, press gently, wanting to know how I can keep writing in all this. I (like to) imagine you are truly curious how I find the energy. But do I also sense a mild reproof?

What you're receiving, then, is an exercise in flaneur-ship. It is meandering, circuitous, and also overcaffeinated and sleep deprived. (Maybe right there is the answer?) You're going to have to bear with me. This is a letter blindly stumbling through mysteries—and the mystery your question presents remains preeminent in my mind. But none of this will likely provide you the answer you need. The best I can do is throw up a few signposts or a cairn like the ones you stumble upon on a particularly arduous hike, warning you that the trail is forking.

The first mystery is why, when I received your email, I thought immediately of punctum and studium and a Beatles song. I would forgive you if you wrote back criticizing me with the admonition that punctum, studium, and the Beatles' "A Day in the Life" mashed together as the subject line of an email forms nothing more than a word salad. There exists, categorically, no apparent similarity. And in truth, at some point, all that punctum, studium, and the Beatles' song had in common is that I was thinking about each one simultaneously, and if you know me by now you are aware that it is entirely possible for me to mull entirely contradictory ideas for no apparent purpose and to no good or useful end.

But here is the truth of any bricolage: you stare long enough and you begin to find meaning. I *believe* there is a connection. You see, all three are in some ways, perhaps indirectly, about grief—or more precisely about the mystery of our grief reaction. Why we do and don't feel grief when experiencing a work of art.

I deliberate on this not because I'm a particularly grief-stricken person, but because as a writer, by necessity, I traffic in grief. I package it. I sell it. Honestly, I use it in hopes that it will make my work stand out across the transom, at the reading, or when someone with only twenty-five dollars is trying to decide which book to buy. As an editor, I always tell writers eager to submit that they should send in a polished work, spelling and grammar-checked, formatted properly. Honestly, I'll not only forgive ½-inch margins and typos on every page but champion that story or essay, if it makes me really feel something. I can fix typos. I cannot give you heart.

The mystery here then is why, at certain moments, in certain stories do I feel grief. I often have some shallow, cursory answer. I can give you a fairly pat answer as to why the Beatles' song "A Day in the Life" makes me sad. I know why an essay that referenced the novel *Rings of Bright Water* moved me enough that I wrote a special note to the chief editor: *Accept this one, please.*

I even think I understand why the moment in the trailer from Episode 6 of the 2019 television version of *His Dark Materials* when the young female protagonist who spookily resembles my niece commands another character "Fight" makes me want to burst into tears. I now know why, after nearly thirty years of periodic research, a very short segment from Holst's *Jupiter, the Bringer of Jollity* causes me to weep every time I hear it.

And by grief I mean something that is intense and acute but also finite, that spiraling sensation we experience at moments of loss or agitation but that we also are aware will subside eventually. Sadness, sorrow, and particularly depression, may not ever end without intervention. Grief, however, isn't something to be frightened of. We associate grief with belief—think of the feeling of listening to a hymn even if you're not Christian— with love—every parent is aware of this—with awe, and most importantly profundity. Also, the grief reaction associated with art is very particular and also safe. I have had stories reduce me to sobs, but I would only facetiously claim that such a story "ruined my day." In the end, I'm grateful.

I want to make clear that grief is not the only emotion that art makes us feel. Art makes us feel awe. It makes us laugh. It makes us feel joy. It makes us appreciate beauty as Kant and Hegel contend. Holst, when he wrote Opus 32. IV, *Jupiter, the Bringer of Jollity,* meant it to invoke a great national pride in a beleaguered nation. But I'm fascinated by grief because I suspect—though I have no real proof of it—that almost all of European and American aesthetics has evolved from an acute moment of grief experienced while watching a play.

Let me put it his way. I often forget that Western aesthetics, with its focus on the study of beauty in art, is actually not the study of the creation of art but the study of the reception of art. Because of that, philosophers, critics, artists themselves have sought to locate, quantify, and set the perimeters for our emotional connection to art. Probably the first actual attempt to name and define this quality for ancient Greek art is Aristotle's use of the word *catharsis*. What is surprising is that for the reach of the concept of catharsis—it's important, for example, to psychotherapy—it actually only makes up two lines in *Poetics*. Catharsis appears in Aristotle's definition of tragedy and he associates catharsis "with incidents arousing pity and terror, wherewith to establish the catharsis of such emotions." There are other references to catharsis in other works by Aristotle, but he never again seems to fully attempt to define it.

(Yes, you're right. I've anticipated you. Plato writes about pathos—as does Aristotle. But for my purposes here, pathos is a term I associate with rhetoric and, yes, I'm aware that rhetoric is often categorized as an art and that the contemporary essay in its many forms has its roots in rhetoric, but I'm still going to kick pathos out because in this brief moment I get to set the parameters.)

My understanding is that catharsis for the Greeks of Aristotle's time has two connotations. The first is that of medical purgation—getting rid of, expelling from the body, poisons, toxins, humors—and the healing that could subsequently come about from that process. The second is that of purification in the spiritual, religious sense. There appears to be a great deal of argument between people far smarter than I whether or not Aristotle intended us to infer both meanings. But I'm a 21st-century fiction writer and essayist and as such I'm happy to entertain the idea that he meant us to infer two separate things at once—that catharsis is both a physical process and a spiritual process—because I find this both elegant and true to my own experience.

If my logic is clear enough then you can tell where I'm leading us. Catharsis for Aristotle, is a quality of literature that results in a deep and acute emotional reaction. And it doesn't include joy or love or even humor. Aristotle must not have been a very funny man because, as you're aware, in *Poetics,* he does not have much use for comedy. Catharsis is a concept he attaches particularly to tragedy, and he contends that the resulting physical and spiritual cleansing gives tragedy a moral weight that comedy lacks. Catharsis is an effect of tragic work, and I believe that means that for Aristotle the cathartic effect comes by the end of a play as part of the total experience of the play—a sort of tragedy is good medicine.

By the way, when I made that comment about all of European aesthetics being based on one man's grief reaction I was thinking of Aristotle's reading of *Oedipus Rex*, the play that Aristotle references when defining *tragedy*. Aristotle doesn't use the word *grief*, and I don't know if there is an ancient Greek word for grief. But I allow myself the imaginative leap because I am not a scholar of Classicism and while we name single emotions—emotional reactions are certainly a complicated mix of emotional responses. Anyway, it's clear that this play moved Aristotle deeply and profoundly and like so many of us he wanted to understand why.

There are, for me, two main problems with catharsis as the primary concept for defining emotion in art. The first is that Aristotle originally applied it to literature and, specifically, to narrative. For me, that dual meaning of both purging and purification also implies a process, something temporal, and so it's easy to associate it with narrative which is in itself about a temporal process. It's harder to apply to the visual arts—museums would be entirely unnavigable spaces if we were being purged and purified by every other painting we looked at. I realized yesterday, as I was meditating on this lecture, a favorite song may be the only artform that the majority of us return to repeatedly, and naturally, again and again over decades. I love *Moby Dick* but I'm probably not going to return to it, ever. "I was older then I am younger than that now" felt like a promise at twenty. It's a truth for me today. That realization was slow and creeping and did not entail catharsis.

The other problem with the concept of catharsis is that it doesn't reference the mini-moments of emotion in any work of art. I'm not talking about the intense rush of feeling but the little moments of piquancy that help prep us for something larger and help us earn the eventual purification.

And, of course, this all focuses on entirely Western aesthetic. This completely ignores wabi-sabi or rasa or any other great non-Western tradition. There's no mention of queer aesthetics, a tradition deeply important to me. And yet all of these do seem to have in common a desire to understand, and question, how we form a connection to art.

Which brings me to punctum and studium. You already know that both are from Roland Barthes *Camera Lucida*. For Barthes, studium is, very simply, a well-composed image that a viewer appreciates but does not remember later. Barthes uses, as an example of studium, most newspaper photographs. What is important to understand is that studium, as an effect, is an accomplished cohesive, well-designed photograph. Punctum, on the other hand, is a disruptive force. Punctum disrupts the order and elegance of studium. Here's a quote (you knew I was going to do this!): "Punctum is . . . sting, speck, cut, little hole—and also a cast of the dice. A photograph's punctum is the accident which pricks me (but also bruises, is poignant to me)."

The word *accident* here is important. The punctum that Barthes experiences while viewing the photographs in the first half are tied to specific objects in the photographs—for example the pair of Mary Janes a young girl is wearing in a family portrait—but this isn't a rehashing of Eliot's objective correlative because the photographer isn't responsible for the presence of those shoes. Punctum is added to the photograph by the viewer and is not the product of the intention of the photograph. As he writes, "Whether or not it is triggered, it is an addition: it is what I add to the photograph and what is nonetheless already there."

Here's the funny thing about all this. Despite the prominence of *Camera Lucida* in the visual arts, it's a shit text if you
want to actually learn how to take a good photograph. Barthes
isn't interested in the history of photography, the innovation of
great photographers like Bresson or Man Ray. Barthes actually
says he doesn't care about the rules of composition or the reasons we take photographs. Sometimes he doesn't even seem to
like photography. A photograph for him is actually a form of
destruction: "I then experience a micro-version of death . . . I
am truly becoming a specter." (Which makes, by the way, Instagram a graveyard—or better yet a haunted house.) It's also shit
as a craft text. Punctum is a "cast of the dice"? Is an "accident"?
That's something akin to your poetry mentor saying to you in
the first workshop, yeah throw some words together and good
luck.

And, in fact, I think *Camera Lucida* is a trojan horse of an
essay. It looks like an academic treatise on aesthetics but, in
truth, it's a grief-stricken meditation on loss and it's in the second half that the essay finds its beating, aesthetic heart because
it's in the second half that Barthes reveals what has really moved
him to write this essay—a few years before he lost his mother
and he decides to riffle through some photographs of her and
he is surprised by the impact of these photographs on him. And
here is what is most important to me. There exists one photograph in particular of his mother as a young woman. He recog-
nizes his mother in her, but this image is also not the mother he
knew. "It was not she, and yet it was no one else. I would have
recognized her among a thousand other women, yet I did not
'find' her. I recognized her differentially, not essentially. Photography thereby compelled me to perform a painful labor;
straining toward the essence of her identity, I was struggling
among images partially true, and therefore totally false."

For me, I had that experience—or a mini-version of that experience—not when I saw the photograph of Barthes mother—I

never knew her young or old—but when I came upon the photograph of Bob Wilson and Philip Glass. In the version I was reading, the photograph comes after the text referring to it and this is the recreation of my *actual* reading process before I encountered the photograph: *Words, words, words, words . . . Oh, whoa.*

What surprised me is that as a someone who has been in some form of the arts from an early age I've grown up with Robert Wilson and Philip Glass. And Robert Wilson and Philip Glass, in my mind, have always been old—even when they were most likely the age that we are now. In my mind, they are solidified as eminence grise and yet here they both are young, and frankly quite beautiful. I recognize who they are, but I have never had the capacity to imagine them like this. And while I certainly don't feel the grief of a child recognizing his deceased mother, I do feel a twinge. Punctum.

I acknowledge that up to now I haven't made a good case for any of this in a time of catastrophe. We pedal in grief as artists. Do we need to add more of that to the pot when so many are suffering?

To really answer your question about the importance of what we're doing I want to turn to music, and not literature, because the emotional impact of music is nearly universal, crosses cultures, and has also been well studied and well documented. As Oscar Wilde writes (in "The Critic as Artist" if you want to read for yourself):

> After playing Chopin, I feel as if I had been weeping over sins that I never committed, and mourning tragedies that were not my own. Music always seems to me to produce that effect. It creates for one a past of which one has been ignorant, and fills one with a sense of sorrows that have been hidden from one's tears.

And, I think, I hope, you have had this experience when listening to a piece of music because it really *is* extraordinary. But,

I also wanted—just like Barthes—to answer why I feel this way. One of the reasons is rooted in the brain itself. What we identify as single emotions—sadness, horror, terror, joy—are actually rooted physical responses generated from our limbic system and from nowhere else. And maybe—and this is absolutely theoretical—that part of the "surprise" of feeling emotion when listening to music, or reading a book, or watching a play is that we perceive the experience as visceral and primal, maybe even irrational. And, yet, we now know thanks to research in neuroscience that emotion and reason are actually connected to each other. Patients who experience damage to this part of the limbic system also lose the ability at self-organization. They cannot order their lives or their memories.

Ellen Bryan Voigt in *The Art of Syntax* mentions a book by Robert Jordain, *Music, the Brain, and Ecstasy*, which I tracked down and read entirely on a long train ride. Here's a passage from it that struck me.

> At any given moment, our brains can process only a tiny slice of the torrent of experience that comes our way: our bodies can carry out only one action of the hundreds possible: our intellects can model only the fragment of reality amidst infinite possibility. . . . A nervous system must always be on the lookout for the most important activities to which to devote itself. This is the ultimate purpose of emotion.

What I remember most now is Jordain's explication of the role that emotion plays in motivation and goal orientation. We drive forward for something anticipating a certain reward and that reward carries with it an emotional response. The example that he uses, and it's a simple one so I'll use it here, is that you reach into your wallet anticipating that you will find a ten-dollar bill there. If you find the ten-dollar bill there, you will most likely not feel anything at all and in fact never reflect on the moment. However, if you don't find it, you will feel anger and frustration. If you find a twenty-dollar bill you didn't expect, you will experience joy and maybe even awe at your good fortune. But here's what's important: the emotional response is generated in each case by the deviation.

Music works it seems in a similar fashion. It creates anticipation and deviation. We are trained—even if we are not musicians—to hear certain pitches, chords, scales and anticipate what will happen next. Of course, the emotion comes not from regularity. Jordain writes the following:

> Musical expression is forever at odds with musical structure. Every deviation from an anticipation tend to weaken subsequent anticipation and thereby undercut the impact of further deviations. A momentary shift in tempo brings a tinge of emotion, but at the price of undermining the overall sequence of rhythmic anticipations that keep a piece moving along. When too many deviations fall together, the listener loses track of the underlying meter and ceases to anticipate coming beats forcefully. Similarly, using too many non-scale tones (chromatic tones) tends to obscure tonal centers so that harmonic resolutions lose their impact.

Which brings me to the Beatles. Part of my love for the Beatles is that the songs are a connector. I remember hearing them as a young child in England in the '70s, and I have very precise images that I associate with particular songs. But, maybe, my favorite Beatles song is "A Day in the Life."

When I started this, I was fully intending to do an entire analysis of the song. I was going to discuss at length Lennon and McCartney's decision to slow the tempo for the opening. As an actual musician, you can check me on this—and I welcome that—but the tempo of the Lennon section is 72 bpm.

The average pop song is something like 116 bpm. I was going to mention the "Oh boy"—I read the news today, "Oh Boy,"—could be heard as a reference to Buddy Holly's very popular song "Oh Boy—you know all my love, all my kissing. And the tempo of *that* song is 100 bpm. I could mention the suicide that John Lennon describes in the first verse is a reference to an actual suicide that devastated British culture and politics at the time. In fact, the song's lyrics tackle the writer's—in this case Lennon's—inability to participate in the ritualized and communal grief of his fellow countrymen. But I also realize that at nearly over 4,000 words this is already a *long* email.

Because this email already goes on a bit long, I will now limit myself to singling out that line that everyone thinks is a reference to drugs—which I'm sure it is. Personally, I have long just dismissed the line as a tongue in cheek come-on by a group of randy blokes—an acknowledgement that even when the rest of the nation is grieving this is all certain young men are thinking about. But then, when I mull over why this song mattered so much it occurred to me that "A Day in the Life's" elaborate, avant-garde structure is all of these things and also this. It's an acknowledgement that many of the things that are supposed to cause us grief—particularly events and rituals that demand grief—have little effect. And the song is a wish: in the face of all that inures us in our everyday life to grief and emotions I'd love *this* song to turn you on. Make you feel something. It is an elaborate rethinking of what a pop song really is—the slowed tempo, the reference to a suicide, World War II, potholes—is done in the hopes that it makes you to *feel*.

So why does any of this matter? Well, maybe because art is the emotional analog to physical exercise. My father, when he was still well, explained to me that in the here and now exercise is a terrible thing to do to your body. The simple act of running—at any speed—causes microfractures in your bones, muscle tears, your mind which already burns an enormous amount of calories just processing the world, now has to go into full gear to keep you a) upright and b) help you to tune out the information you don't need and take in the information you do need so that you can escape the saber tooth tiger at your heels. But, my father stressed, that it's what comes next that is invaluable. Exercise causes microstress to our bodies, but our bodies then go into full gear to heal all this mini-trauma. If you exercise regularly enough you are training and preparing your body to continuously heal itself—and if you start early enough this process will continue well into what we consider old age. In other words, by causing manageable mini-traumas we are prepping our bodies to handle the real traumas—viruses, actual broken bones and torn ligaments, cancers—to come.

I contend, that art—and here I mean all art, not just literature—prepares us for the emotional battles to come. It allows us to experience rage, horror, joy, excitement safely and then learn to manage those experiences in such a way that they create meaning for us. It also helps us to survive. I don't like to think of myself as old, and I'm technically not, but I have lived long enough to assure you, with no doubt that that which will destroy you, you will not see coming.

I believe *this* is a necessary endeavor in the face of all that is coming, that we cannot see, and that will happen despite our lack of imagination and the best we can do is prepare ourselves and each other in the moment.

On this, I hope we might agree . . .

I'd love to turn you on.

Truly, h.

NOTES

The following works were essential in writing these essays:

"Broken Arrow"

Dobson, Joel. *The Goldsboro Broken Arrow: The B-52 Crash of January 24, 1961, Goldsboro, North Carolina: The Story of the Men on the Sharp End.* J. Dobson, 2011.

Laplace, Pierre-Simon De, and Andrew I. Dale. *Philosophical Essay on Probabilities.* Springer, 1995.

"The Night Hydrogen Bombs Fell Over North Carolina." 29 May 2012, https://www.ourstate.com/hydrogen-bombs-north-carolina/

Schopenhauer, Arthur, David Carus, and Richard E. Aquila. *Arthur Schopenhauer: The World as Will and Presentation.* Prentice Hall, 2011.

"Lady"

Ellmann, Richard. *Oscar Wilde.* New York: Knopf, 1988.

Reich, Jeffrey M., MD, and Richard E. Johnson, Ph.D. "Microbacterium Avium Complex Pulmonary Disease Presenting as an Isolated Linglular of Middle Lobe Pattern." *Chest,* vol. 101, no. 6, June 1992, pp. 1605–9.

Rubin, Bruce K., MD. "Did Lady Windermere Have Cystic Fibrosis?" *Chest,* vol. 130, no. 4, Oct. 2006, pp. 937–38.

Wilcox, Elaine Wheeler. "Women of Ceylon." *National Magazine*, vol. 37, no. 5. February 1913.

"In the Presence of God I Make This Vow"

Bennet, Eve Tavor. "The Marriage Act of 1753: A Most Cruel Act for the Fair Sex." *Eighteenth Century Studies*, Family Values in the Age of Sentiment, vol. 30, no. 3, Spring 1997, pp. 233–54.

Billington, Jeff. "US soldiers 'shop' on Craigslist for wives to get more pay, benefits," *Today*, 22 Oct. 2014, https://www.today.com/news/us-soldiers-shop-wives-get-more-pay-benefits-2D80186882.

Davis, Rebecca L. "Not Marriage at All, but Simple Harlotry: The Companionate Marriage Controversy." *The Journal of American History*, vol. 94, no. 4, March 2008, pp. 1137–63.

Daybell, James, ed. *Early Modern Women's Writing, 1450–1700*. Palgrave Macmillan, 2001.

Wall, Alison. "For Love, Money, or Politics: A Clandestine Marriage and the Elizabethan Court of Arches." *The History Journal*, vol. 38, no. 3, Sept. 1995, pp. 511–33.

"Pretty Girl Murdered"

Jayawardena, Kumari. *Feminism and Nationalism in the Third World*. Verso, 2016.

Tambiah, Stanley J. "The Structure of Kinship and Its Relationship to Land Possession and Residence in Pata Dumbara, Central Ceylon." *The Journal of the Royal Anthropological Institute of Great Britain and Ireland*, vol. 88, no. 1, 1958, p. 21, DOI: 10.2307/2844073.

"Confessions of a Dark Tourist"

Bloom, Mia. *Dying to Kill: The Allure of Suicide Terror*. Columbia University Press, 2007.

Ely, Alfred. *Journal of Alfred Ely*. Edited by Charles Lanman. D. Appleton and Company, 1862, http://www.archive.org/stream/journalofalfrede00elyauoft/journalofalfrede00elyauoft_djvu.txt

Sharpley, Richard, and Stone, Philip R. *The Darker Side of Travel: The Theory and Practice of Dark Tourism.* Channel View Publications, 2004.

Thiranagama, Sharika. *In My Mother's House: Civil War in Sri Lanka.* University of Pennsylvania Press, 2011.

Woolf, Leonard. *Growing: An Autobiography of the Years 1904 to 1911.* Harcourt Brace Javonovich Publishers, 1961.

"Amblyopia: A Medical History"

Davis, Lennard. *Obsession.* Amsterdam University Press, 2009.

Pfaffenberger, Bryan. "The Kataragama Pilgrimage: Hindu-Buddhist Interaction and Its Significance in Sri Lanka's Polyethnic Social System." *The Journal of Asian Studies,* vol. 38, no. 2, 1979, pp. 253–70, DOI: 10.2307/2053418.

Shield, Todd. "Ford Sued Nationwide Over Alleged Part Defect." *Washington Post,* 20 Oct. 1996, www.washingtonpost.com/archive/politics/1996/08/20/ford-sued-nationwide-over-alleged-part-defect/c0c35adf-b7dc-4cb4-8b56-7da61532c20c.

Simon, Linda. "Unjust Were the Ways of Milton." *New York Times,* 16 June 1991, www.nytimes.com/1991/06/16/books/unjust-were-the-ways-of-milton.html.

Sorsby, Arnold. "On the Nature of Milton's Blindness." *British Journal of Ophthalmology,* vol. 14, no. 7, 1930, pp. 339–54, DOI:10.1136/bjo.14.7.339.

University of Wisconsin-Madison. "'Lazy eye' may bully the brain into altering its wiring." *ScienceDaily,* 25 August 2015, www.sciencedaily.com/releases/2015/08/150825111141.htm.

"Soft Target"

Adams, Rachel. "'A Mixture of Delicious and Freak': The Queer Fiction of Carson McCullers." *American Literature,* vol. 71, no. 3, Sept. 1993, pp. 551–83.

Hitt, Jack. "Dawn." In *Dawn.* National Public Radio. 28 Feb. 1996.

Rich, Adrienne. "Compulsory Heterosexuality and Lesbian Existence." *Signs: Journal of Women in Culture and Society,* vol. 5, no. 4, 1980, pp. 631–60, DOI: 10.1086/493756.

Schulman, Sarah. "McCullers: Canon Fodder?" *The Nation,* 26 June 2000.

"Six Drawing Lessons"

Krauss, Rosalind. "'The Rock': William Kentridge's Drawings for Projection." *October—MIT Press,* vol. 92, 2000, pp. 3–35.

"Punctum, Studium, and the Beatles' 'A Day in the Life'"

Jourdain, Robert. *Music, the Brain, and Ecstasy.* HarperCollins, 1998.

Schaper, Eva. "Aristotle's Catharsis and Aesthetic Pleasure." *The Philosophical Quarterly,* vol. 18, no. 71, 1968, p. 131, DOI:10.2307/2217511.

21st CENTURY ESSAYS
David Lazar and Patrick Madden, Series Editors

This series from Mad Creek Books is a vehicle to discover, publish, and promote some of the most daring, ingenious, and artistic nonfiction. This is the first and only major series that announces its focus on the essay—a genre whose plasticity, timelessness, popularity, and centrality to nonfiction writing make it especially important in the field of nonfiction literature. In addition to publishing the most interesting and innovative books of essays by American writers, the series publishes extraordinary international essayists and reprint works by neglected or forgotten essayists, voices that deserve to be heard, revived, and reprised. The series is a major addition to the possibilities of contemporary literary nonfiction, focusing on that central, frequently chimerical, and invariably supple form: The Essay.

---

*Annual Gournay Prize Winner